Modern Guide to
MUDRAS

About the Author

Dr. Alexandra Chauran, of Port Moody, Canada, received a master's degree in teaching from Seattle University and a doctorate from Valdosta State University. She is the author of dozens of books, including *Crystal Ball Reading for Beginners*, *Have You Been Hexed?*, and *Getting Through It*. In her spare time she enjoys streaming on Twitch as QueenOfDiamonds and chatting with readers.

Modern Guide to

MUDRAS

CREATE BALANCE AND BLESSINGS IN THE PALM OF YOUR HANDS

Alexandra Chauran

Llewellyn Publications
Woodbury, Minnesota

FIRST EDITION
First Printing, 2021

Cover design by Kevin R. Brown
Interior Mudra illustrations © Wen Hsu. Other interior art by the Llewellyn Art Department.

Llewellyn Publications is a registered trademark of Llewellyn Worldwide Ltd.

Library of Congress Cataloging-in-Publication Data
Names: Chauran, Alexandra, author
Title: Modern guide to mudras : create balance and blessings in the palm of
  your hands / Alexandra Chauran.
Description: First edition. | Woodbury, Minnesota : Llewellyn Publications,
  2021. | Includes bibliographical references. | Summary: "Modern Guide to
  Mudras teaches how to use hand gestures for worship, meditation,
  spellcasting, sacred movement, and ritual storytelling"— Provided by
  publisher.
Identifiers: LCCN 2021033546 (print) | LCCN 2021033547 (ebook) | ISBN
  9780738767666 (paperback) | ISBN 9780738767765 (ebook)
Subjects: LCSH: Magic. | Gesture—Miscellanea. | Gesture in worship. |
  Meditation. | Mudrās (Buddhism) | Mudrās (Hinduism)
Classification: LCC BF1623.G47 C43 2021 (print) | LCC BF1623.G47 (ebook)
  | DDC 133.43—dc23
LC record available at https://lccn.loc.gov/2021033546
LC ebook record available at https://lccn.loc.gov/2021033547

Llewellyn Worldwide Ltd. does not participate in, endorse, or have any authority or responsibility concerning private business transactions between our authors and the public.

All mail addressed to the author is forwarded but the publisher cannot, unless specifically instructed by the author, give out an address or phone number.

Any internet references contained in this work are current at publication time, but the publisher cannot guarantee that a specific location will continue to be maintained. Please refer to the publisher's website for links to authors' websites and other sources.

Llewellyn Publications
A Division of Llewellyn Worldwide Ltd.
2143 Wooddale Drive
Woodbury, MN 55125-2989
www.llewellyn.com

Printed in the United States of America

Also by Dr. Alexandra Chauran

Dedication

This book is dedicated in gratitude to my peerless guru, M. Subhashini Vijay Santhanam of From Within Academy, who first taught me the power of mudras. I continue my studies with the hope that I will achieve perfection in them.

Disclaimer

This book is not intended to provide medical or mental health advice or to take the place of advice and treatment from your primary care provider. Readers are advised to consult their doctors or other qualified healthcare professionals regarding the treatment of their medical or mental health problems. Neither the publisher nor the author take any responsibility for any possible consequences from any treatment to any person reading or following the information in this book.

Contents

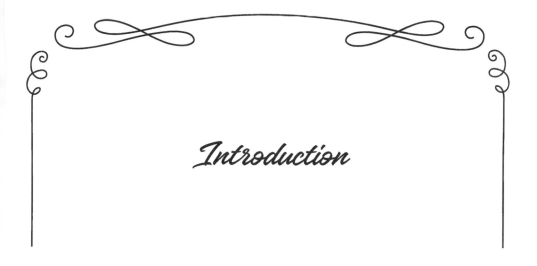

Introduction

Imagine filling your life with the grace and joy of hand gestures and movements that captivate your subconscious. Mudras are symbolic, ritual gestures meant to evoke a state of consciousness and to manifest change in the world. You can learn the secrets of one of humanity's oldest forms of magic, meditation, and wordless communion with spirit through mudras. The only tools you need are those you take with you wherever you go, the powers of your own hands. Place your hands one way to calm down after a stressful day at work one evening, or perhaps use another gesture to invoke fertility before trying for a baby. Use a simple sign to ward off the toxic feel of a creepy coworker. Though mudras are no substitute for medical or mental treatment, the possibilities are as endless as the richness of the cultures that discovered them.

Mudras are sacred hand poses and gestures that can be used in the contexts of worship, meditation, spellcasting, sacred movement, and ritual storytelling. Through simple exercises, you will be able to invoke blessing and shut down negativity at home, at work, and when adventuring out in the world. Mudras will speak to you if you have ever wanted to add a bit of color and beauty to everyday life without having to invest in candles, crystals, and incense. They can be beautifully ostentatious or discreetly covert.

Many practical applications will be drawn together in this down-to-earth guide. As your author, I have trained for years in a Hindu temple dance called Bharatanatyam, which always makes heavy use of mudras during its practice. I have a master's degree in teaching, so I enjoy carefully scaffolding lessons so that any reader can pick up the book and build on concepts they learn from the ground up, chapter by chapter. The chapters in this book were written to be read in order, since some ideas build on others. If you do choose to jump around, please refer back to the first chapter for full descriptions and demonstrations of the mudras used, since that's where I'll get you started right away. I hope you are as excited as I am to start sharing the powerful magic of simple hand gestures and poses. Everyone can find at least one practice that will become an important personal key to empowerment and inner peace.

A Brief History

The word *mudra* is Sanskrit in origin and means "gesture" or "seal." The primary intent behind mudras is to seal spells or blessings. Mudras are typically taught as an oral tradition, since the ability to record video of gestures is relatively recent in human history. Technically, a mudra can be done with the entire body, but the vast majority of people use only the hands. It is certain that humans have been using their hands for storytelling and magic before recorded history began. Traditional mudras are generally understood to be Indian in origin but, of course, every human culture has hand signs and gestures of significance. For example, Buddhist mudras are expressed within Japanese martial arts. I studied Shōrin-ryū karate at the competitive level and found that mudras were often contained within the memorized series of poses called *kata* that often resemble a dance or ritual.

In Tahitian hula dance, mudras are used to honor and respect the natural world by representing, for example, the trees or the ocean. According to Hawaiian legend, the gods of our creation (Kane, Lono, Kū, and Kanaloa) used mudras when reciting incantations, which explains the origin of hula dance. Many dance forms feature hand movements and poses to catch the eye. My first dance teacher was a belly dance teacher. She taught that the fundamental theorem of dance is to isolate movements to one part of your body at a time. She asked her students to imagine a ball of glowing green goo in their hands and to stick that goo to different parts of their body. Wherever the glowing green goo is, you focus your attention and your movement. That dance teacher's methods weren't very different from magical theory. Magic is the art of making your will a reality. Spiritual energy is the life force of the universe and the engine that governs magic. Mudras are movements that grab that energy, which you can visualize as glowing green goo if you like. This can direct your attention and intention inward or outward.

Mudras are used extensively in five forms of sacred Indian temple dances. There is one form of dance for each of the spiritual elements: Kuchipudi for earth, Mohiniattam for air, Bharatanatyam for fire, and Odissi for water. There is a fifth form that represents spirit or sky called Kathakali. I trained and helped teach Bharatanatyam for years and studied its mudras. In Bharatanatyam, mudras are used for dramatic storytelling, emotional expression, and invocation of various deities. Each class begins with prayer and a specialized series of mudras that bless and thank the earth and our teachers as well as invite blessings from the divine. Mudras are also used in Indian yoga practices and are depicted in Hindu and Buddhist art.

In the Mediterranean, one must be careful about how one holds one's hands. There are gestures that are harmless in many cultures that can be an insult or a curse in the Mediterranean region. I will go more into detail in chapter 4, in the section called "Malevolent Mudras and How to Counteract Them." There are also many aboriginal cultures around the world that use their hands in dance and storytelling. There is even a Crow Sign Language that can be used to speak entirely with hand gestures, very much like the more common American Sign Language (ASL).

Mythology and Legend

The world of fine art is full of meaningful hand poses, especially when it comes to spiritual themed art. The position of hands of a deity or holy person can evoke memories of specific myths and legends or can impart blessings. The next time that you see a painting or sculpture of gods, saints, orisha, lwa, or other sacred beings, pay attention to how they are holding their hands.

Their hands tell the story of their myths. Their hands bless the viewer. So much meaning is wordlessly conveyed through the hands. Many of the Indian dances I learned carried out the myths. In one, I represented Shiva dancing and giving blessings to the audience by holding my right hand up to them with a bent elbow and thumb aligned with fingers. In another dance, I invoked Ganesh into the temple by holding my hands as he would with his ritual objects, at the sides of my belly as if I had his large belly.

A Word about Cultural Appropriation

I wanted to conclude this introduction with a serious point about respecting other cultures while learning from them. While it is true that nobody holds a copyright on how to hold or move their hands, many of the spiritual practices contained in this book have drawn inspiration from other cultures. When I was taught sacred mudras by the Indian community, I spoke with members about their feelings about Western culture adopting spiritual practices. On the one hand, many with whom I spoke were proud that Indian customs were suffusing Western culture, especially for the benefit of those of Indian descent who felt disconnected from their roots. On the other hand, it is viewed as distasteful to take a spiritual practice from another culture and use it in a disrespectful way.

For example, I was taught to wear a bindi, a red dot to symbolize my sacred headspace, on my forehead. My teachers approved of me wearing a bindi in performances, dance class, and even out into the world after my dance class, carrying Shiva's blessing with me. However, those same teachers would not approve of the fad of club-goers in the UK wearing bindis on their foreheads decoratively for a night of drinking heavily and partying. If your intention is pure, you are using it in the appropriate context, and most of all, if you listen to those who speak from their culture of origin and express its importance to them, you can address and reduce harmful cultural appropriation. Cross-cultural dialogue about race, identity, and spirit should be an ongoing thing for all of us, not something to be dodged or explained away.

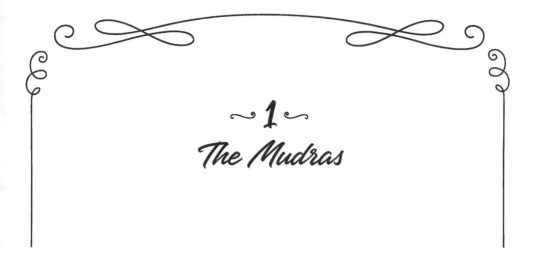

~1~
The Mudras

I am beginning your mudra journey with mostly static poses since it may take a while to get the hang of some of them. Consider the difference in flexibility between different bodies. Some people can touch their toes easily, while others may struggle to touch their knees. Whatever your body can do is fine. Your mudras may look different from someone else's due to age, flexibility, disability, injury, or level of experience and practice. Consider that most people who are flexible enough to do the splits were unable to perform the stunt the first time they tried. Most people who can do the splits had to practice stretching exercises, at least for weeks, before they could gradually work up to the full splits. Likewise, there are some mudras here that I struggled to master. I practiced them daily by running through them once or twice in the morning and before bed. I would also practice the hard ones throughout the day, like when waiting in my car at a red light. I just want to stress that you should never beat yourself up if your mudras don't look like someone else's. Our bodies create their own personal expressions of our inner and outer beauty. Don't worry about looking wrong while you're developing your practice. By the end of this chapter, you will be able to integrate mudras into your life by posing your hands in specific ways during seated meditation.

Mudras and Meaning: The Language of Mudras

It would be impossible to contain all the world's mudras in one book, so I'm just going to include a selection here that can be important building blocks when choreographing a ritual, choosing a meditative pose, or casting a spell. This book incorporates a mix of ancient mudras that you'll see named in Sanskrit and modern mudras noted in English. All the mudras that are used in later chapters of this book will be introduced here, so you can refer back to this chapter whenever you need a refresher on how to perform a mudra or when you are writing your own spells and rituals. It is my hope that you will eventually memorize them all and take them with you wherever you go, but for now you can choose just one or two to integrate into your life. I also had to be selective about the interpretation of the mudras since, as with any art form, interpretations can be endless. You might even find new meanings to ancient mudras on your own. I tried to include only the more practical interpretations so as to reduce confusion and make this easier for the beginner.

How to Use Mudras to Create Meaning in Your Life, Worship, and Meditation Practice

Before we dive into the actual mudras, I want to give you some context for how you will use them. There are two basic categories of mudras, one-handed mudras (asamyuta hastas) and two-handed mudras (samyukta hastas). The mudras that only require one hand are ideal for rituals, spells, and exercises when one must use the other hand to hold an object or when you must be discreet with the mudra in a pocket or behind your back. Traditionally, statues and paintings often depict one-handed mudras with the right hand, and you might find they feel more powerful when done with whatever your dominant hand may be. Ideally, however, just like with fitness exercises, you should alternate and practice with either hand so that they are both trained well and balanced.

Two-handed mudras are sometimes used in spells, rituals, and exercises but are perfect for using in meditation, since holding the hands in a still pose can also help quiet the mind. If you have a disability that makes two-handed mudras difficult, the one-handed mudras are quite sufficient for meditations. As you look through the mudras in this chapter, try to follow along to see which mudras are easy for you to form with your own hands. Start with using the easiest ones in the meditations and rituals included in this book. Begin practicing the more difficult ones until they come easily to you.

Placement of the arms is important too. What you do with the rest of your body depends upon context and ability also. In general, if seated or standing, you should hold your hands in front of your chest about a foot in front of you, or half if you have shorter arms, and keep your elbows up and level with your hands. But if you are doing a ritual, you can move your hands freely as needed. If you are meditating for a long time, you may rest your hands on your knees or relax your elbows inward. Many wise sages are said to have held mudras for extremely long periods of time in uncomfortable positions.

One-Handed Mudras

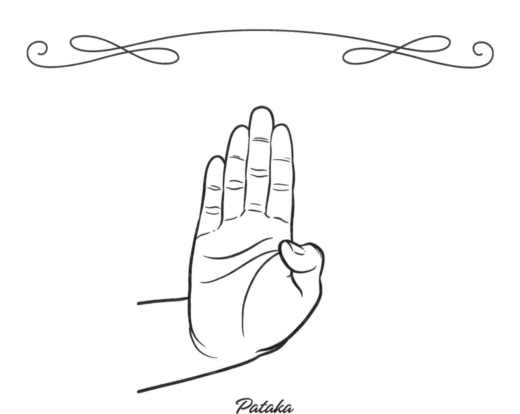

Pataka

To make this mudra, keep your hand flat and make sure that your thumb is always tucked to the side of the hand. It can be tricky to remember to keep your thumb in. It's okay if your hand is slightly curved, but keep it as flat as you can. Pataka usually represents a flag and can be used in exercises that represent pride of land or nation. Practitioners of martial arts will also recognize pataka as the knife hand used in karate and many other fighting forms, so pataka can also represent protection or defense. Some other translations of pataka may be "as a cloud" or "forest." Pataka is very commonly used in greeting or blessing.

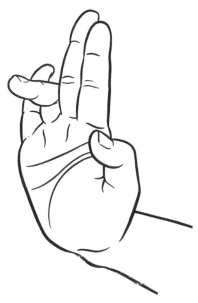

Tripataka, a.k.a. Surya and Spiritual Freedom

Tripataka represents three flags, a crown, or a tree. It is formed by holding your hand flat, tucking the thumb in, and then folding the ring finger over so that it sticks out perpendicular to your hand. This mudra was the hardest for me to learn because that ring finger just would not behave for me. I had to practice it for quite some time. It's okay if your ring finger curves during this mudra, but hold it as straight as your body allows. This mudra can be used over your head as a crown to represent "putting on a different hat" if you want to bring a new job role into your life, especially a leadership one.

If you hold down the top of your ring finger by pressing down on the whole finger at the first knuckle with your thumb, this mudra becomes surya mudra. Surya represents the sun, and it is possible to raise your body temperature using surya. It is used to increase appetite and is even thought to ward off sickness. When used with both hands, tripataka becomes the spiritual freedom mudra, helping you connect with the limitless power of spirit to help yourself or others.

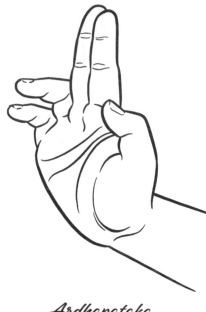

Ardhapataka

Ardhapataka represents a half flag or two banners. Form pataka and then lower your ring and pinkie fingers to make this mudra. It can represent leaves, a writing surface, a knife, a tower, or the horn of an animal, or it can simply indicate two things together. This mudra can be useful during meditations to protect or prolong a new relationship. When representing a writing surface, the shikhara mudra is often used to represent the writing tool with your other hand. You will read about shikhara later in this chapter. When the thumb is connected to the ring and pinkie fingers at the tips or the nails, ardhapataka becomes a version of the prana mudra, the more common form of which is described next.

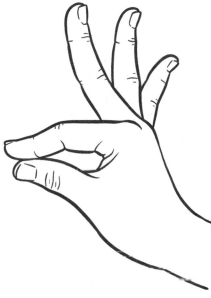

Hamsasya, a.k.a. Prana

This common mudra, hamsasya, also called the prana mudra, is made by touching your pointer finger and thumb together and splaying the rest of the fingers as if you were to delicately pluck a flower. Literally "swan's beak," this mudra has many uses. You can use it as if to light a lamp or a beacon to guide your way somewhere or to guide someone else's way to you. You can also use this in a tying thread motion to seal a spell or to do knot magic when no cord is available for you to tie a symbolic knot. You can use hamsasya to imitate drawing or painting. I have seen it with two hands, moved up and down the torso to represent inner spirit. When used in meditation, this mudra is believed to restore the movement of spiritual energy within the body to produce a healing effect for the spiritually afflicted. Ironically, it can also help with excess hyperactivity by allowing that energy to flow with greater volume. Think of the prana mudra as if you are turning an energy spigot so that the energy flows like water, faster and more intensely, so that you can use it any way you wish. The prana mudra can add an extra boost to the end of any prayer or spell. It can also be used in meditation to increase psychic vision.

Kartarimukha and Crossed Fingers

Kartarimukha represents scissors, and you can see why. It looks remarkably like the scissors hand used in the game rock paper scissors, also known as roshambo. For this mudra, your ring and pinkie fingers are held by your thumb and your pointer and middle fingers are held apart, with the pointer finger behind the middle finger. Keep your palm facing away from your body with the wrist bent to hold as a pose. This mudra is often used in a scooping motion that will be used in a later ritual for cutting ties with someone toxic in your life (see page 192). This mudra can represent the separation of a couple, lightning, or an opposing force. It is a powerful mudra and thus can also represent death. If you cross your fingers, as you might have done behind your back as a child to excuse a white lie, this mudra becomes a sign for warding off evil and welcoming luck.

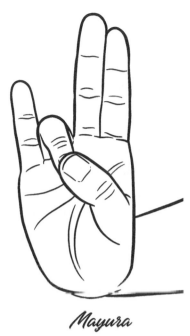

Mayura

The mayura mudra represents a peacock. To make this mudra you must hold your ring finger down with your thumb and hold the rest of your fingers straight up, though sometimes the remaining fingers are splayed open. This mudra is often accompanied by a waggling motion at the wrist to represent the trembling of a peacock's feathers when they are on full display. Mayura can also represent the combing or separation of hair, fame, or putting a bindi on one's forehead. This mudra, as you might guess, represents beauty. It can be used in glamour spells, which are those that allow others' perceptions of you to change for the better.

Ardhachandra, Chandrakala, and the Sign of the Goddess

These three mudras all represent the moon. While ardhachandra represents a half-moon and thus things in one's life that are on their way to coming to fruition, it can be used to boost spells, or it can consecrate or bathe an image or object. To make ardhachandra, hold your hand flat, palm outward, with your thumb at a 90-degree angle to your hand, all on the same plane. If you hold both hands in ardhachandra and then frame a magical drawing or sigil that is lying on an altar or table, you can charge it with your energy. Both ardhachandra and its crescent moon aspect, chandrakala, can be used to denote a source or new beginning. To form chandrakala, hold your index finger and thumb to form a letter L shape, with the back of your hand facing you. All three mudras can be used to enhance meditation, prayers, and any contemplative practice. I remember when, about twenty years ago, the modern moon mudra, or sign of the Goddess mudra (along with the sign of the horns), was one used for witches to signal to each other that they were also of the old religion. To form the sign of the Goddess, curve your index finger and thumb into a letter C shape, with the back of your hand facing you. Another version of the sign of the Goddess can be done by extending the pinkie and thumb to the sides of the hand while keeping the rest of the fingers curled into a fist, as in the "hang loose" sign that surfers use.

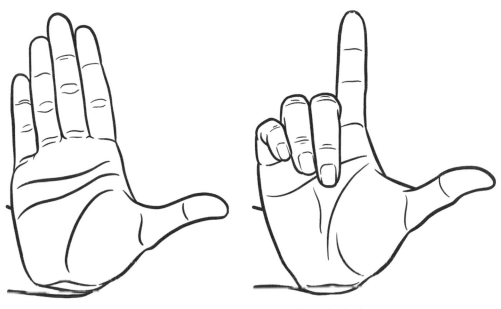

Ardhachandra   *Chandrakala*

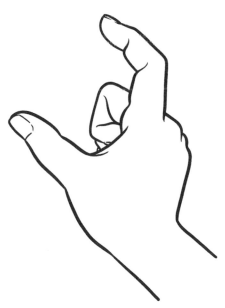

Sign of the Goddess or Modern Moon Mudra

Arala

The arala mudra is just pataka with the pointer finger bent. It can represent wind when it is waved back and forth like a flag. It can also represent holding a bottle that you can tip to your mouth as in a drinking motion. The symbolism of arala can be used to represent taking something into your body, which can be useful in spells for healing, confidence, or any other inner state that you wish to achieve. There are some exercises that you can do with arala in the section called "Spells for Everyday Life" on page 127.

Shukatunda

Shukatunda is a difficult mudra to hold, as it is the pataka mudra with the pointer and ring fingers bent perpendicular to the hand and the palm facing away from you, held upright at the wrist. The literal meaning of shukatunda is "parrot's head," but the mudra often represents the act of shooting an arrow or throwing a spear. Due to the symbolism of projection, shukatunda is a good mudra for sending a spell. This mudra is also used by mystics when they speak magical words, so it is excellent for use during invocations.

Mushthi, the Fig, Azabache, and Pressing Thumbs

Mushthi is simply a fist with the thumb pressed in on the outside of the fist. You might also recognize this as the rock from the game of roshambo. It does represent either combat or being steadfast like a rock. Thus, this mudra can be a very protective sign used in protection spells, especially when the index finger knuckle is pushed out to protrude in a form called azabache, and can also represent stick-to-itiveness if you are performing a mudra exercise to keep a job, relationship, or housing situation just the way it is. The mushthi mudra also represents grasping and holding on, so it can be used for exercises meant to bring love or money your way so that you can catch that energy and bring it into your life. When the thumb is tucked between the index and middle fingers, mushthi becomes the fig, a gesture used to ward off the evil eye. When used two-handed with the thumbs tucked into the fist, mushthi becomes the pressing thumbs gesture for good luck.

Shikhara

Shikhara looks like the thumbs-up sign and can be used in greetings or blessings. It has varied meanings, including references to combat as a bow or tooth. It can also represent writing as a writing implement when waggled back and forth as if drawing with a pen in your grasp. In meditation, shikhara can help with memory when you try to recall a specific event or time. Shikhara can represent a bell that you ring if you move it as if grasping a bell, and it can thus substitute for a bell in banishing and exorcism magic.

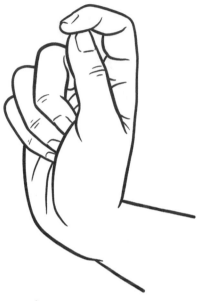

Kapitta and Bherunda

You may have seen the goddesses Saraswati and Lakshmi holding this pose, and this sign can be used to invoke goddess energy. For the simple form of this mudra, hold your hand in a fist but with your thumb up and capped with your index finger. A more advanced version raises the ring and pinkie fingers as far as your body will allow. For Ganesh invocations, this sign can be used held outward from the body as if you had Ganesh's big belly and can represent the sacred symbolic objects he holds: the conch to call to prayer, a rope to control the wandering mind, or an axe to sever unnecessary attachments. In dance, I have used this mudra to represent a love bird, and the kapitta mudra can be used in love magic. Kapitta can also represent lighting incense or a candle, and it can be used in situations where real incense and candles cannot be used.

When both hands are forming kapitta, the mudra becomes bherunda, which often represents two lovebirds together but may have originally represented a mythological bird with two heads. As such, bherunda can be used to invoke magical power and destruction.

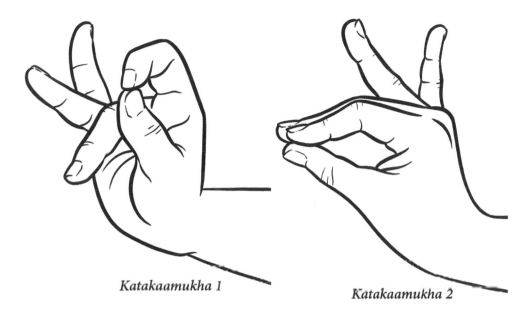

Katakaamukha 1   *Katakaamukha 2*

Katakaamukha

This common katakaamukha mudra is similar to the OK symbol but with the pads of both the middle and forefinger touching the thumb. Some people press the thumb flat onto the finger pads to make a straight slope of the fingers, but I was trained to use this mudra with a gentle curve between the thumb and the fingers. The mudra resembles a deer's head, and it can also represent flowers or holding a necklace or bracelet for glamour magic when it is used in its two-handed mudra form. The two-handed mudra form can also be held crossed at the wrists. This mudra can transform into another version of katakaamukha, done by sliding your thumb inward to press against your hand and curling your index finger around it (as in kapitta) and then allowing your middle finger to bend down a little further so that it is perpendicular to your palm. The latter form of katakaamukha can represent a bird or a lotus.

Suchi and the Sign of Silence

The suchi mudra is to hold your index finger upright as if one has an idea or a point to make. The suchi mudra is believed to have healing properties because it is thought to cleanse the body and mind. Holding the suchi mudra may elevate your vibrational energy signature, so this pose can be excellent for meditation. You can read about the Lesser Mudra Practice in chapter 2, which is a meditation that can use suchi (see page 85). When held to the lips, suchi becomes the sign of silence, representing discretion and mystery. Be cautious, as the pointed finger can be offensive in some cultures, so keep that finger pointed to the sky and away from other people.

Padmakosha and Kangula

The padmakosha mudra is a very feminine gesture and can be used to invoke feminine energy. Make the padmakosha mudra by holding your hand palm up and then extending all your fingertips and thumb upward as if a mango were being held aloft by your hand. It often represents holding a fruit of some kind, and so it can be used to take into the body the energy that you want fruiting in your life. This hand also represents a lotus, hibiscus, or any other flower and can bring peace and well-being through meditation. Like shikhara, padmakosha can be a substitute for a bell when no bell is available for banishing or exorcism rituals. Padmakosha can also represent an egg or a new beginning, so when held as a pose it can stimulate creative energies in your life. Kangula looks like a slightly more challenging version of padmakosha, as the hand is held in the same manner but with the ring finger pressed down into the palm. The meanings of kangula are the same; however, the bell meaning implies wearing a string of bells. For this reason, using kangula to symbolize hanging a necklace or anklet of bells can protect the wearer.

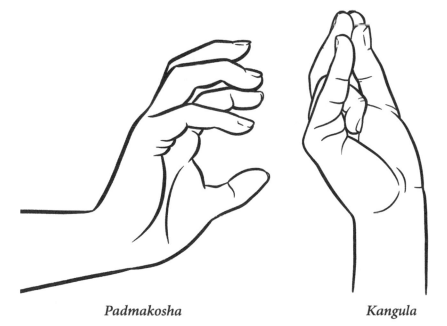

Padmakosha   *Kangula*

Sarpashirsha

The literal meaning of sarpashirsha is a serpent. Form sarpashirsha by holding your hand upright with the fingertips curled over so that your hand represents a cobra's hood. The sarpashirsha mudra is often in motion, so try waggling your hand from side to side as you slowly lower your hand a bit. The serpent represents eternal life. The shedding skin of a snake can represent a new start in your own life. The mudra can also represent the gift of a water offering to the divine and can be used in place of an offering when none is available during worship. The two-handed form of this mudra is done by crossing the hands at the wrists to represent two snakes intertwined.

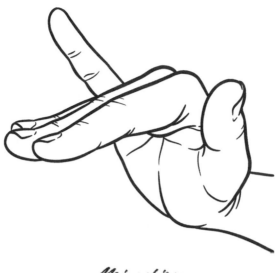

Mrigashirsa

Mrigashirsa is made by holding the hand at a right angle with the thumb and pinkie held outward. The remaining fingers are sloped downward. This is a very feminine mudra because it resembles a uterus and fallopian tubes. This mudra can be useful for calling beloved female ancestral spirits to visit and protect you. When made with both hands, this mudra can invoke the god Krishna. This mudra can also be used in meditation to concentrate on areas of your life that are controlled by fear or conflict so that you can contemplate and dispel all fear.

Simhamukha, a.k.a. Apana, and Modern Sign of the Horns, a.k.a. Sign of the God

Simhamukha and the sign of the horns resemble each other, so I wanted to point out their differences. Simhamukha is made by pressing the middle finger and ring finger against the thumb to make what looks like a hand puppet with ears. The sign of the horns is made by holding the middle finger and ring finger down with the thumb against the palm of the hand, and it can represent a horned god. These signs have different meanings, but both can be used to increase psychic vision. Simhamukha means "lion" and can be used to summon courage, especially when facing an illness, since it can also represent the preparation of medicine by a doctor or pharmacist. Simhamukha is also thought to remove toxins from the body and aid the health of the liver when taken into an extended meditation for forty-five minutes. Simhamukha also represents a sacrifice burned in fire and can be used in lieu of a fire offering in situations that do not permit fire. The sign of the horns represents masculine energy and can be used to ward off curses, especially when presented with horns pointed downward and waggled back and forth.

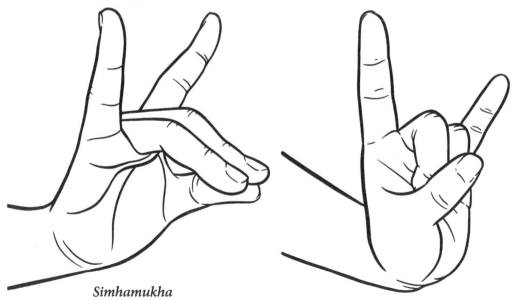

Simhamukha

Sign of the Horns

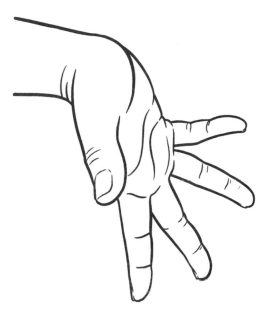

Alapadma

Alapadma is a beautiful mudra that represents the lotus in full bloom or the full moon. Hold your palm flat and splay the fingers with the pinkie and ring finger pointed upward and the rest directed as far back and downward as your body allows. This mudra can be used to accept blessings, especially from the moon. This mudra can be used to represent beauty in glamour spells. You can move this mudra, allowing it to unfold toward parts of your body to which you would like to apply its influence. When held up like a hand mirror, alapadma helps you see your own beauty as well.

Chatura and Hansapakshika

You can make the chatura mudra by first bending your fingers forward at a 90-degree angle, lifting your pinkie, and then folding your thumb underneath the hand. The pinkie is pointed upward, but the rest of the fingers should be held perpendicular to the palm and sloping downward. This mudra is especially used for blessing the earth by touching earth and for blessing your own eyes by holding this mudra up to cover your eyes. Chatura symbolizes the treasures from the earth, such as gold, copper, or iron. This mudra can be used in grief meditation to feel your grief and to process through it. This mudra is also a good one for glamour spells, especially when changing the way that you see things. Hansapakshika is different from chatura in that the thumb is tucked to the side of the hand instead of underneath in the palm. Hansapakshika represents a swan's wing and the number six, but it can be most useful by representing a bridge whenever you want to meditate on opening up the bridges of communication between yourself and someone else.

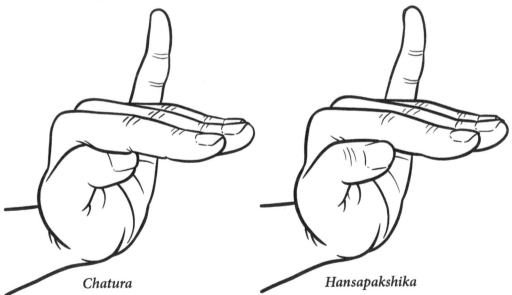

Chatura   *Hansapakshika*

Sandamsha and Mukula

Sandamsha is a mudra that only makes sense when it is in motion. The tips of the fingers and the thumb are tapped together as if imitating a pincer. This mudra can be used to represent offerings made to deities and is another great mudra to use if you have nothing on hand to actually offer spirit when worshiping the divine. This mudra also represents the number five and can be used to express and offset anxiety. Mukula means "bud," but it was taught to me as representing a mouse. Mukula is formed by making the closed form of sandamsha and sometimes waving the tips of the fingers back and forth as if your hand were a scurrying mouse. The mukula mudra represents eating and is thought to aid digestion. Mukula can also be used in love magic when representing the arrows of the god of love, Manmatha.

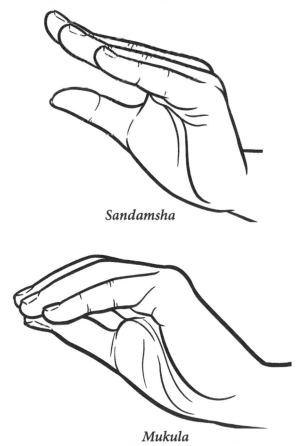

Sandamsha

Mukula

Tamrachuda

Literally meaning "rooster's head," tamrachuda is made by making a hook with your index finger and keeping the rest of your fingers in a fist. In dance, I was trained that this was used to touch the face to represent a beauty mark on an exceptionally beautiful woman. For this reason, tamrachuda can be used for glamour spells for physical beauty. Tamrachuda can also be used when you want to draw attention to something that you have made with pride, such as a business proposal or a painting, that you want to bring to the attention of a customer.

Trishula

Literally meaning "trident," trishula is identical to the hand sign you might make to represent the number three. The number three is sacred in many different faith traditions. For example, it can represent the holy trinity of Brahma, Vishnu, and Mahesh or the three aspects of the Goddess: Maiden, Mother, and Crone. The goddess Durga is a fearsome protector goddess who carries a trident, and the mudra can be used in a stabbing gesture to ward away enemies.

Vyagraha

Form vyagraha by making a claw hand. This gesture is often used in dance to represent the powerful goddess Durga to invoke her protection, since she is often depicted with a tiger. Use this mudra when you want to protect yourself or children. Think mama bear energy. This mudra can ward off negativity and defend you against negative magic.

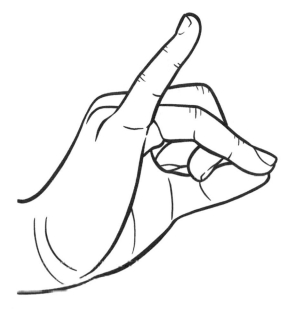

Modern Simplified Mudra for the Lungs, a.k.a. Modern Bronchial Mudra

Taught to me by my dance guru, Subhashini Vijay Santhanam, during the 2020 COVID-19 pandemic, this mudra is meant to strengthen your lungs in preparation for some stressor. To make this mudra, press the tips of your index, middle, and ring fingers into three points on your thumb so that you can feel the pressure. This mudra is best practiced for fifteen minutes a day, either one hand at a time or two-handed, to ward off respiratory illness.

Hridaya, a.k.a. Heart

Hridaya is very similar to the modern simplified mudra for the lungs, but the index finger is curled tightly into the palm and the ring and middle fingers are aligned next to each other to both meet the thumb at its tip. This mudra is believed to aid heart health. Use this mudra when you need to vent emotions that weigh heavily on your heart. If you feel yourself becoming angry or afraid during a conflict, use this mudra discreetly to restore composure. Taking this mudra into meditation helps you gain peace from conflicts within your own heart.

Two-Handed Mudras

Any of the one-handed mudras can be used as two-handed mudras simply by making both hands create the same pose. Choosing what hand displays the mudra depends on its use. If you do not need to hold anything else, make the mudra with your dominant or active hand. If you need to hold something while making the mudra, you may need to use your passive or nondominant hand out of necessity, and this is okay too. Some of the two-handed mudras double the one-handed mudras and add to the richness of their meaning. Other two-handed mudras are unique themselves. You don't have to wait until you've mastered the one-handed mudras before moving on to try two-handed ones. Some of the two-handed mudras may be easier on your hands than their one-handed counterparts. Give them a try.

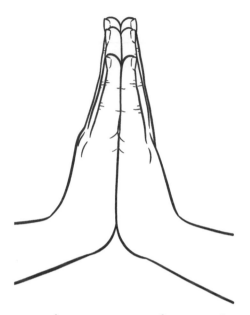

Anjali, a.k.a. Namaskara or Modern Salutation Seal

Anjali is used as a greeting or in prayer and is simply the palms pressed together. Hold your elbows up if you can, but some bodies don't want to bend at right angles at the wrist, and that's okay. You may have heard of the greeting "namaste," which is commonly associated with a bow and the anjali mudra. When done together, this greeting roughly means "I recognize that the divine in you is the same as the divine in me." Use this mudra to honor the divine within and the divine all around you. This mudra can also be used in place of an offering when you have nothing else to offer.

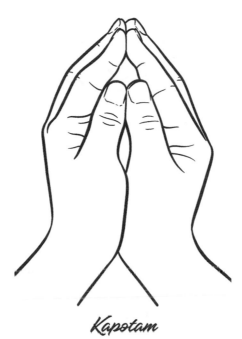

Kapotam

Kapotam mudra is made by first forming anjali and then tenting your hands while keeping your thumbs together to create a pocket of air between your palms. This mudra can be used in greeting as a sign of respect. It represents respectful conversations, acceptance, and obedience. It can be held to aid studying for an exam, and it can be held to evoke a practical and pragmatic attitude toward a situation.

Karkata

Karkata is made by interlacing the fingers together but keeping the hands straight. Literally, karkata means "crab." In dance, this mudra represents the arriving or coming together of people. It can also represent bending, as a branch or when stretching. This is a sign of both vulnerability and compromise.

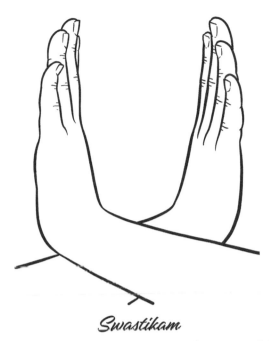

Swastikam

This gesture is also called the swastika, but it has none of the evil of the Nazis' use of the swastika symbol. Swastikam simply means "crossed," and so this mudra is when your hands are held upright in pataka and then crossed at the wrist. Sometimes, this mudra is associated with the crocodile. Swastikam can be used to denote a spiritual obstacle or a path that has been blocked. This mudra can be used for binding and unhexing, as it represents the imprisonment of energy.

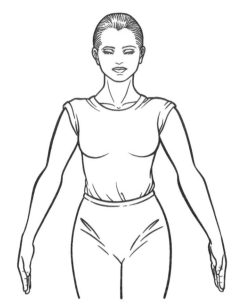

Dola and Modern Goddess Stance

This mudra requires a specific pose from the body and cannot easily be performed sitting or kneeling. Dola is performed standing with arms gently lifted outward from the body to form an A and hands held in pataka and gently bent at the wrists. Dola can be extremely calming when you form it by bringing your hands down and then allowing the wrists to flop the hands as they relax. When palms are faced outward, this can also be "Goddess stance," representing the divine female energy of the universe.

Pushpaputa and Modern Yoni

Pushpaputa is simply cupped hands. A more advanced version of this mudra uses flat hands in pataka that are not pressed together but are simply angled toward one another at the tips of the fingers as if holding a tray. Pushpaputa represents an offering of flowers to the divine and is often performed while kneeling. Use this mudra to seek emotional balance or calm extreme emotions. The yoni mudra is similar, but with slightly spread fingers and with the pinkie and ring fingers of your right hand overlapping the two of your left hand (see next page). The yoni mudra invokes goddess energy, represents the cauldron of death and rebirth, and stimulates creativity while making room in your life for abundance. The yoni mudra can be used in a pinch to aid concentration and awareness. A more advanced yoni mudra is done by interlacing the fingers at the first knuckle, tenting your index fingers, and then touching your thumbs together to tent them in the opposite direction of your index fingers (see next page).

Pushpaputa

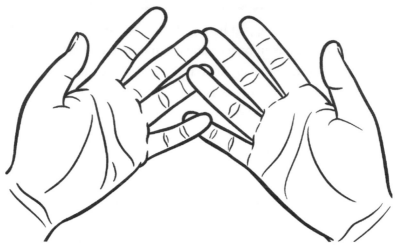

Yoni

Advanced Yoni

Shivalingam

Shivalingam is one sacred sign of the god Shiva and is formed by holding your right hand in a thumbs-up gesture and then moving it around your flattened left hand from below to rest on its palm. Though this gesture is essentially masculine, it also represents the union of male and female energies. Use this powerful mudra to gain self-confidence and to energize your body and mind toward action. This mudra can also boost intuition and calm the mind, and some even use it for weight loss.

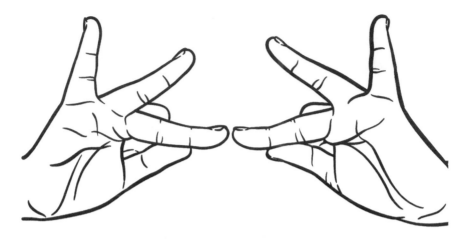

Shakatam

I use wide eyes in dance with this mudra, which is formed by touching your thumb and middle finger together and curling your index finger up into your palm, extending the ring and pinkie fingers splayed. This mudra transforms your face into a devil's face, with teeth shown by your curled fingers. Thus, this can be a defensive and protective mudra to frighten away negative energies.

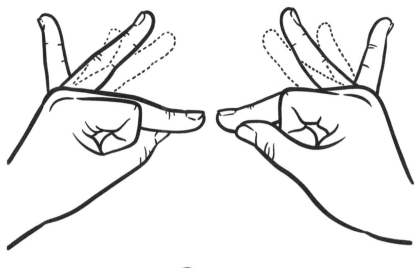

Bramara

The bramara mudra is made by turning the shakatam mudra on its side and vibrating the pinkie and index fingers as if your hands were the wings of a bee. This beautiful mudra can also be moved gently up and down as you vibrate the wings to invite positive and industrious springtime energies into your life. It is believed that this mudra can alleviate allergy symptoms, but no mudra can substitute for a doctor's help with severe allergies.

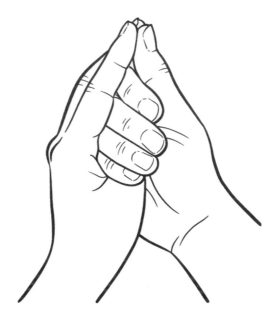

Shankha, a.k.a. Modern Seashell Mudra

Shankha looks like a conch shell, and that is what it's intended to be. Grab the thumb of your left hand and enfold it into the palm of your right hand. This seashell mudra can be used to invoke the sea if the idea of sitting on a beach watching the waves calms you from stress. Because of its association with the cool ocean, the seashell mudra is thought to help calm fevers, rashes, sore throat, and any other burning sensations. Because of the imagery of using a conch shell to sound a horn, shankha can be used at the beginning of a ritual to call to order. There are many health benefits attributed to the seashell mudra, and it can also help you have a clear voice if you must give a speech. It is believed that shankha can heal health problems that occur in the throat if you can manage to chant "om" while meditating for fifteen minutes.

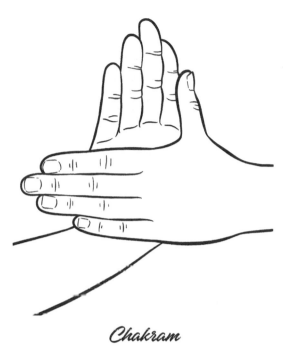

Chakram

Literally meaning "wheel," the chakram mudra can be made by holding hands flat with the thumbs out but fingers pressed together and
then holding your palms together with your hands at right angles to
one another. This is no ordinary wheel but a representation of the
divine weapon of Vishnu. Holding this mudra or moving your hands
by rotating your palms can increase your personal energy and even
extend your aura, your own personal energy signature, farther outside
your body.

Pasha

Pasha is made by linking your index fingers together and then holding your hands one above another vertically. If used during dancing,
this mudra is accompanied by an angry face because it represents an
argument. It is reminiscent of the American Sign Language sign for
"problem" and also resembles a chain. Use pasha mudra when trying
to prevail during a disagreement or when meditating over a problem
to seek wisdom and strength.

Kilaka

Kilaka is the same as pasha but linking the pinkie fingers instead of the index fingers. Opposite of pasha, kilaka is accompanied by a peaceful expression and sometimes a happy head wobble when dancing. This is because kilaka represents loving interactions, fun conversations, and sharing joy and laughter with someone else. Use this mudra when trying to seek peaceful resolution to a disagreement with a loved one.

Samputa

Samputa mudra is made by cupping your hands together as if you were holding a butterfly. This mudra's meaning is a secret or a treasure. Use this mudra to awaken the divine self-value within. Since samputa can allow you to trust your higher self, it also aids communication when you have to speak your own truth. Meditate with samputa mudra to get to know your true self. Since samputa can also represent a casket, it is excellent for use with shadow work, which includes exercises to get to know your dark side and the destructive powers of death.

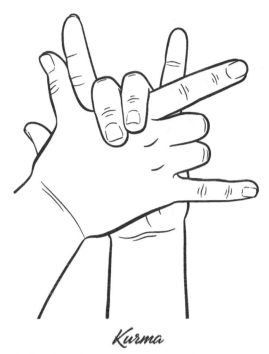

Kurma

Kurma is made by first forming samputa, then pressing your palms against one another and extending the thumb and index fingers of both hands. When done correctly, kurma represents a turtle or tortoise. Spiritually, this mudra represents the god Vishnu. Meditate with this mudra to call upon your inner perseverance or for protection. This mudra represents stability of the body, mind, and soul.

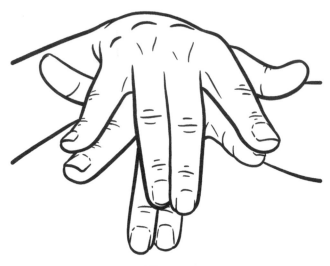

Varaha

Just as the sign of the horns can ward away a hex, varaha is another protective mudra. Place your hands on top of one another with palms down and thumbs extended to the sides. Now lower the middle and ring fingers of both hands to form the snout of a warthog with your other fingers representing horns. The god Vishnu took the form of a wild boar to save the world, and you can evoke that heroic energy in yourself with this mudra.

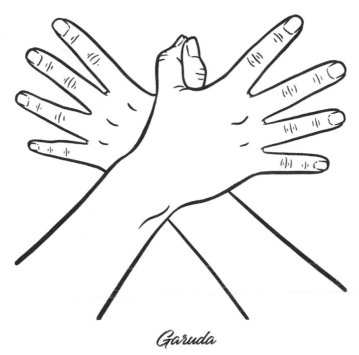

Garuda

Literally meaning "eagle seal," this mudra looks as if you were trying to make a bird shadow puppet. With thumbs linked and fingers splayed with palms toward yourself, you can even make the wings flap to complete the mudra. Use this mudra to find inner freedom, just like the eagle that Vishnu rides in myth. Not only can this mudra be used to increase your own freedom to choose, but it can also evoke a powerful advocate from within you to help others find freedom. The eagle seal can also help you with discipline and steadfastness.

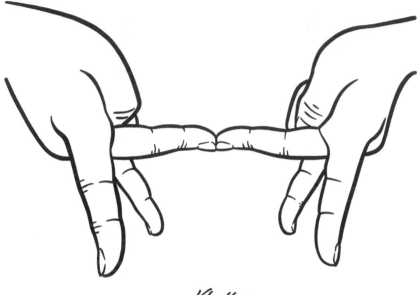

Khattva

Literally meaning a "bed" or "cot," khattva is a bit of a challenge to make with your hands. Touch the middle fingers together to make the mattress of the bed, your pinkie and index fingers make the bedposts, and your thumbs are tucked in at the head and foot of the bed. Use this mudra in meditation before bed to aid healthy sleep. If you are a busy person who doesn't take to rest well, using this mudra can signal your brain to just stop and live in the moment. Invoke dreams with this mudra.

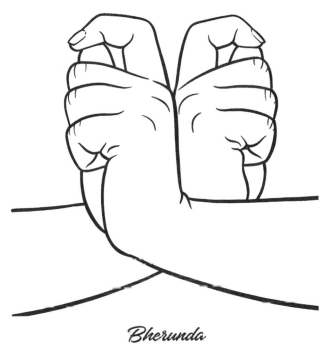

Bherunda

In the bherunda mudra, two birds or two bird heads are shown by folding the index finger around the thumb to form a beak and allowing your fist to be the rest of the bird's body. This mudra is done with crossed wrists to mean "terrible," but another version can be done by holding the hands together without crossing wrists, to show two lovebirds for magic with companionship. Another, more advanced bird mudra that can be done one-handed or two-handed is made by forming bherunda and then raising the ring fingers and pinkie fingers to form the wing and tail feathers of the birds.

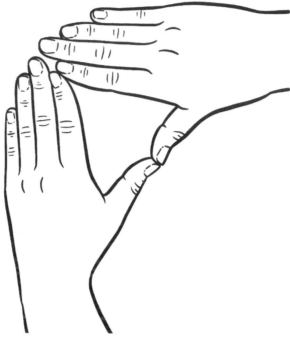

Modern Triangle of Manifestation

This triangle mudra is a modern mudra that I learned through Wicca. The triangle mudra originated in Italian witchcraft and is formed by simply making a triangle with your index fingers and thumbs and holding the rest of your fingers in line. The triangle is a symbol of the Goddess and of union between the Goddess and the God. This mudra is traditionally used held in front of the belly. When held in front of the face, this mudra focuses energy, and when held over the head, it is used for summoning.

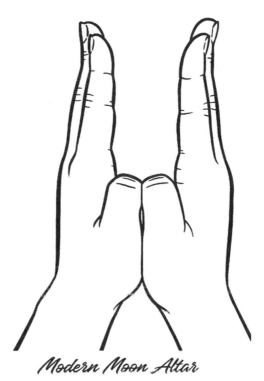

Modern Moon Altar

The moon altar mudra is done by holding your hands next to one another with palms flat toward one another. Fold in your thumbs and press them together so that they form a flat altar. This is used when the full moon is in sight by holding the hands so that the moon appears to rest on the altar formed by the thumbs. This mudra is used for drawing divine feminine energy from the moon or for worshipping her when accompanied before or after with two hand kisses thrown to the moon.

Modern Bliss

This modern mudra looks like a heart shape with your fingers. Ideally, you'll be touching the knuckles of your index fingers together, and you'll touch the knuckles of your middle and ring fingers to their counterparts as well. Your thumbs touch to form the point of the heart. Note that a version of this mudra can be done with the thumbs tented upward instead of downward. Meditate while holding this mudra by yourself or seated facing a partner to invoke orgasmic bliss into your life. The mudra represents the union of male and female generative forces to create eternal harmony, but you don't need an opposite-gendered partner, or any partner at all, to reap the benefits of this symbolic union. Using this mudra can cut through distorted energy in cases of physical or emotional pain and can also release spiritual baggage on a karmic level. Soul retrieval can be done with the bliss mudra to integrate back together the parts of you that feel spiritually fragmented. More about soul retrieval can be found in chapter 3. Meditate with the bliss mudra to discover and eradicate negative energies that cause intrusive thoughts. Using this mudra while imagining the energy contained around a diseased part of your body is believed to aid healing by releasing the negative energy and restrictive beliefs that have been afflicting it. Use the bliss mudra along with the prana mudra afterward to combat mild depression.

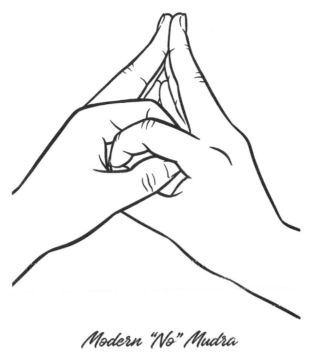

Modern "No" Mudra

The "no" mudra is made by touching the thumb and index finger of each hand but linked together as in a chain. The remaining fingers are held straight to form a triangle. We've all felt at war with ourselves in one sense or another. This modern mudra can help banish any of your desires that do not serve your true self. Rid yourself of intrusive thoughts and block anyone's attempts to manipulate you. You can also use this mudra to block energies from another, such as a curse.

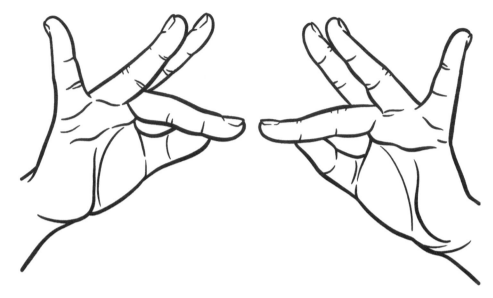

Modern "Yes" Mudra

To form this affirmative mudra, touch the very tips of your thumbs to the inside of the first joint of your middle finger on each hand. Use the "yes" mudra when chanting or meditating upon affirmations or to add a boost for success to any spell. And since this mudra means yes, it can help you decide which option is a yes when you are hesitating upon a choice due to uncertainty.

Atman

Atman is a Sanskrit word meaning "true self." Form this mudra by tenting your fingers and then touching the first knuckles of your middle fingers together. The thumbs touch in a downward position. The atman mudra is especially useful to solve family relationship problems that are causing strife between you and a loved one. Holding the atman mudra can aid the intimacy of your communication as well as bring your heart to a place of agreement and unity. If there is something divisive that is tearing your family apart, you can do your part to restore harmony by meditating with atman daily until the issues at hand are resolved.

Empowerment and Love

This empowerment mudra is formed by pressing the second knuckles of your middle and ring fingers together, while allowing your index fingers and pinkie fingers to tent and touch tips. Gaze at this mudra until you see three triangles. The purpose of this mudra is to integrate all the disparate energies inside you so that you can direct them as you will. If you feel any stuck and unbalanced energies in your body, this is a mudra to take into meditation. The empowerment mudra is also effective against bullies at school or in a workplace and is thought to boost the immune system to stay healthy or aid healing.

The love mudra is a very similar mudra with remarkably different results. Press the knuckle of just your middle fingers together and allow the rest of your fingers to tent, this time touching the thumbs in a downward position instead of upward with the rest of your fingers. Note that the love mudra is also similar to the atman mudra, but the knuckles meet at the second joint instead of the first. Make no mistake, this mudra is not about platonic love. This love mudra can be used in meditation to enhance sexual passion. The love mudra also aids with self-acceptance, but I recommend the following for a self-acceptance mudra without any sexual connotations instead.

Modern Empowerment

Modern Love

Modern Self-Acceptance

Ultimately, this mudra is about self-acceptance, so if you practice it before any activity during which you feel self-conscious, it will bring about positive change. To form this mudra, put your hands together in prayer pose and then curl the pointer finger of your right hand over the curled pointer finger of your left hand to frame the thumbs. Use this mudra as a prayer pose to summon your higher self and make the best decisions. Gain contentment with your current situation and remove self-imposed limitations by meditating with self-acceptance. This mudra can also protect and enhance mantras or affirmations so that they become more meaningful and hold more truth.

Modern Fearless

The fearless mudra is made by tenting your fingers, touching the ring fingers together at the first knuckle, and then resting the tips of those ring fingers on the tips of your thumbs. The fearless mudra is one that you can practice before heading into a job interview if you're feeling nervous. You may find areas in your life that you've blocked out for yourself out of fear of failure or other repercussions. Using the fearless mudra can help you break through self-imposed obstacles. It is believed that meditating with the fearless mudra can aid healing, since chronic anxieties can take their toll on physical health. Please note that the fearless mudra alone will not be sufficient to treat a medically diagnosed anxiety condition.

Modern Prana Integration and Modern Body Integration

We've all felt unbalanced at times: for example, if you were caught off guard with bad news or you're losing your sense of identity due to illness or divorce. The prana mudra can help you feel balanced with a sense that all your spiritual energy is fully integrated with your body's physical energy. By simply folding your hands together and interlacing your fingers like you would if you were a good student waiting at a desk, you've formed the prana integration mudra. Make sure that you practice deep belly breathing when holding the prana integration mudra during meditation. The body integration mudra is for the reverse experience—that is, when your body feels disconnected from your mind and spiritual energy, which can easily happen after surgery or any sort of encounter that makes your body feel violated.

The body integration mudra is formed by holding your hands together at the third knuckles with fingers folded flat against the palms and thumbs touching at the tips. The purpose of this mudra is to align your spiritual energy with your physical form. Some believe that the alignment of one's own power with the body can aid anything from healing to weight loss. This mudra can also be used to ground and center yourself so that you feel more calm, alert, and present where you are.

Modern Prana Integration

Modern Body Integration

Modern Soul Vibration and Modern Trust

Before you can find your tribe or your soul mate, you must know yourself. The soul vibration mudra is formed by touching the first knuckle of your last three fingers while touching the tips of your index fingers and the tips of your thumbs. Hold the soul vibration mudra to get in tune with your own personal energy signature. If you become adept at meditating with soul vibration until you can sense your own energy strongly, you may be able to use this mudra to share energy with a partner. The trust mudra is identical to the soul vibration mudra, except your last three fingers connect at the second knuckle instead of the first. Use the trust mudra in partnered rituals or meditations. The trust mudra can also be used before working to seek out a trustworthy person for platonic or romantic relationships or for business dealings, such as a mechanic, lawyer, or realtor.

Modern Soul Vibration

Modern Trust

Ganesh, a.k.a. Modern Patience, and Modern Hookup

Form the Ganesh mudra by linking your hands together, with the fingers of each hand enfolded into the palm of the other and thumbs tucked in. The Ganesh mudra is ideal for using in self-hypnotism to anchor your consciousness to any feeling that you can conjure up inside your head, especially feelings of security and harm reduction. In meditation, the Ganesh mudra can also be used to remove obstacles in your life and to enhance your own patience, steadfastness, and perseverance. If you need to open your heart up to become more tolerant or loving, the Ganesh mudra can help you. The Ganesh mudra is excellent for use by children. As a student teacher, I was taught the "hookup" mudra, which helps children and adults alike calm down and sit still while paying attention. To perform the hookup, extend your hands in front of you with thumbs downward and cross them at the wrists so that you can interlace your fingers together. Bring your hands down and toward your stomach, and then raise them up so that the pinkie-side edges of your hands rest against your chest. I'm bad at sitting still to watch educational videos, so I use this mudra to keep me in my place.

Ganesh, a.k.a. Modern Patience

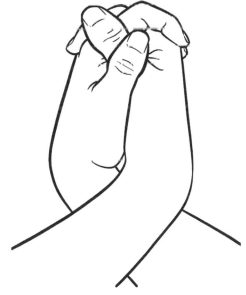

Modern Hookup

Modern Inner Vision

The inner vision mudra is formed by interlacing the knuckles of your pointer and middle fingers, right over left, and then touching your thumbs together. The purpose of the inner vision mudra is to allow yourself to see the truth. Whether you're seeking the pragmatic truth about whether your relationship is disintegrating or seeking the abstract truth of the spirit world as separate from time and space, this mudra will help you attain the wisdom you seek. If consulting on a specific problem with this mudra, hold it for at least ten minutes a day in meditation for two weeks.

Modern Keep It Together

Here's your "emergency" mudra for when you feel like you're mentally falling apart and need some peace and grace in the moment. Pinch your index finger to your thumb on each hand and then hold the pinched hands together, tenting the rest of the fingers. Try holding this mudra for five minutes when you feel upset. You can also take this mudra into meditation on a regular basis in order to inoculate yourself against impatience and frustration.

Modern Abdominal Relief

If you're feeling acute tummy upset, try out the abdominal relief mudra. Hook your index fingers together and touch your thumbs, allowing the rest of your fingers to curl into your palms. Spend three minutes breathing deeply while holding this mudra. For chronic tummy troubles, use this mudra daily for ten minutes, but keep in mind that this just works to ease suffering rather than treat any disease. This mudra is also excellent for menstrual cramps or labor pains.

Trishira

Trishira is Sanskrit for "three of that which carries," and it represents a major trinity of spiritual energy pathways that flow through your body. You can make trishira simply by tenting all your fingers and touching your thumbs together while keeping your palms apart. Think of trishira as activating all the energy highways in your body in order to help you feel calm and alert. Read chapter 2 to learn how to perform a meditation called the Greater Mudra Practice using trishira.

Modern Asthma

I have asthma, and of course I need a rescue inhaler during an attack, but the asthma mudra is a good complementary meditation. For this mudra, your hands are held apart from each other, except the middle fingers are connected at the first knuckle with the rest of your fingers and your thumbs spread out. This mudra is best done after five or six minutes of the lung (or bronchial) mudra (see page 33). The asthma mudra is also good for use during hurried breathing brought on by emotional upset or a panic attack.

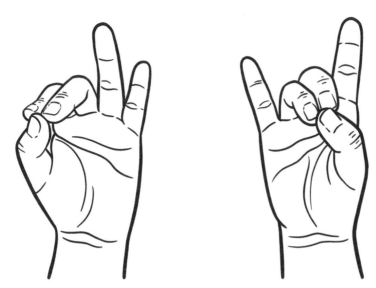

Pushan, a.k.a. Modern Biofeedback

Pushan, literally meaning "nourisher," is the only two-handed mudra in this book that requires that each hand perform a separate and different mudra. Your left hand will form a sign resembling the sign of the horns, except that the middle and ring fingers will touch gently at the tip of the thumb. For your right hand, touch your index and middle fingers to your thumb. This mudra honors the sun god Surya, and it is believed to enhance the nourishment that you receive from food, aid the breathing capacity of the lungs, and soothe nausea or abdominal or pelvic pain.

Mudra Mistakes to Avoid

As mentioned in the introduction, one must always be mindful of the concept of cultural appropriation. Avoid making mudras into a game or a pretense, and always approach them with a sense of reverence. Preparing yourself before meditating or working with mudras in ritual can be done by taking a moment to pray or simply take a few deep breaths. Treat your mudra practice as you would any practice that requires discipline. That means committing yourself to working with the mudras in a serious manner. For example, plan to meditate fifteen minutes a day for a week. Or plan for only five minutes a day, perhaps at the same time each day. It's okay to set reasonable expectations if you can only handle a brief meditation, but follow through with your promises to yourself.

Another potential issue with mudras is that a beginner might accidentally make a rude gesture due to cultural differences. For example, be careful with suchi mudra, as the pointed finger can be used to lay a curse and is considered impolite in many cultures. Shukatunda held backward (that is, with palm facing toward you) can look like a rudely raised middle finger. Likewise, kartarimukha reversed so that the palm is toward the body is thought of as just as rude as the raised middle finger in places like Australia and the UK. It would be beyond the scope of this book to list all the gang signs that could be conflated with mudras, but it is worth noting that, at the time of this writing, white nationalists often pose for photos flashing a sign that looks like hamsasya.

The fig gesture, mano fico, is another sign with mixed meaning, formed by making a fist and sticking your thumb between your index and middle fingers just like the "got your nose" gesture. In some areas of the world it means protection, gifts, and good luck. In other parts of the world, the fig represents lying, refusal, or sex or is simply considered rude because it resembles female genitals. It is best to avoid flashing the fig around since we live in a multicultural society, and it can be viewed much the same as an extended middle finger. Take care, because there are many talismans sold of a hand holding the fig sign, which may be inappropriate to wear in some contexts. If you buy or make such a talisman, wear it as a pendant under your shirt or otherwise carry it with you in some hidden place.

Context is also important when using mudras in public. For example, in Western culture, when somebody crosses their fingers behind their back, it often means the person is lying to or trying to ward off negative energy from the person to whom they are speaking. You can imagine that, if the person could see the crossed fingers behind your back, they would be terribly upset! Similarly, the sign of the horns is used to ward off curses and can be insulting. The sign of the horns is thought by some Christians to represent Satan and should be avoided in church contexts or around those of the faith who may be offended or frightened by the gesture. When used in private, all mudras are appropriate, so long as your intention is pure.

Common Mudras in Everyday Life

Pataka: The flat hand that you use for hand waving in greeting and for putting your face in the palm of your hand when you feel exasperated is a mudra of comfort. In greeting it shows that you hold no weapons and come in peace. For the self-soothing facepalm, it is the touch of a parent, but it is the inner loving parent for your inner child-self that you summon when you are stressed.

Shivalingam: The thumbs-up gesture for approval is so universal that it has gone digital in social media.

Hamsasya or Prana: The OK sign for approval is meant to boost the mood for others and share your own energies of joy and satisfaction. Unfortunately, the power of a mudra can sometimes be misused. The OK sign has, for example, been co-opted by racist groups who use it as a subtle, hidden signal of solidarity by surreptitiously showing the sign in a shared photo.

Anjali: Often accompanied by a bow and the blessing "namaste," prayer hands are a sign of respectful greeting. In many cultures, the mudra by itself or combined with a bow is used frequently throughout the day in every context.

Kartarimukha: There are many variants of an extended two fingers in our cultural lexicon. The peace sign can be used for calm greetings and well wishes. I remember how charmed I was when I first started riding a motorcycle and learned that motorcyclists hold out a peace sign to each other as they pass, often down low. Many people, when speaking, will curl two fingers twice on both hands to create air quotes to add a sense of disbelief to a statement. And when the two fingers are crossed, they become a wish for good luck.

Mushthi: A raised fist often means violence. However, the fist can also be used to express victory with a fist pump.

Suchi: Aside from the pointed finger being used to direct attention to anything or anyone, a raised index finger can be used to indicate that one has an idea or to command attention when one wants to interject something into a conversation. Even though "finger guns" are technically chandrakala mudra, they definitely have more of a suchi energy.

Chakram: Rubbing one's hands together is stylized in the chakram mudra to emphasize the motion that represents the turning of a wheel. Rubbing hands together can also represent dusting off hands to indicate one is finished with something, or it can indicate excitement and anticipation. The emotions felt at endings and new beginnings are consistent with the meaning of the mudra.

Pushpaputa: Asking for something with the beggar's gesture crosses all language barriers. Hands cupped together and extended when empty beg to be filled. When an offering is placed in the hands and extended, without even speaking, you request that the other person take the offering.

Other Ways to Talk with Your Hands

Though they are not directly based on mudras, there are many ways to pepper your conversation with hand signs. Here are some more that you may already be using in everyday life. As you can see, even though it may feel silly to bless or greet someone with a mudra if you are a beginner to mudras, hand signs are already being used every day.

The Hang Loose Sign: From a fist, allow your thumb and pinkie fingers to extend and then waggle the hand at the wrist. This forms a calm greeting similar to the peace sign, often associated with surfer culture.

The "I Love You" Sign: American Sign Language is a deep and rich form of communication that is beyond the scope of this book, but much of it has made its way into common usage among hearing folk. The most recognizable sign is to extend only the thumb, index finger, and pinkie. The "I love you" sign represents the signed letters *I*, *L*, and *Y*.

The Ask for Money Gesture: Rubbing the first two fingers together with the thumb represents money, imitating the handling of coins. It looks similar to the gesture used when crossing oneself, since those three digits represent the trinity from Christian lore.

~2~
Meditating with Mudras

Meditating with mudras is the perfect way to get started using them in a meaningful context. Meditation allows you enough time to practice forming the mudra exactly right with your hands. If some mudras are harder for your body, practicing with them in meditation can help stretch your hands so that they are better able to hold and form the poses. Just like with yoga or any other stretching and posing exercise, practice will allow you to achieve perfection. Meditating with mudras can also help give your hand muscles a workout. For example, recall that katakaamukha is made by pinching the thumb, index, and middle fingers together and letting the pinkie and ring fingers stick out. If you hold this mudra for a long time, you might notice that your "bunny ears" are drooping—that is, the pinkie and ring fingers begin to curl downward as you relax. Over time, you'll build the muscles to be able to hold those fingers straight for extended periods of time even if your body and mind feel totally relaxed at the same time.

Getting Started

Let us begin our meditation practice with your space. Find a place to meditate that is comfortable where you can remain undisturbed for the time that you choose to meditate. Seated meditation is recommended, in a position that is most comfortable for you so that you can focus on your hands rather than the rest of your body. A traditional pose is sitting with crossed legs with the hands resting on the knees, but you can also meditate seated in a chair with your hands resting on your lap. A more active seated meditation pose is with arms raised and elbows extended to the sides at chest height and hands held in front of your chest but not resting on your chest. The active pose is more challenging, but it can also help you sit up straight during meditation and can help you reaffirm your attention to the mudra with each breath you take since you have to maintain focus to hold the positions.

Whether to time your meditations is up to you, and there are benefits and downsides to each option. If you do not time your meditation, you can practice in a way that is comfortable to you as a beginner. With every breath you take, you must consciously choose to continue meditating or to end your meditation, which can feel freeing for a beginner and can allow you to practice forming random mudras until you feel comfortable with them. Timed meditations are often recommended to feel the benefits from holding a specific mudra. Generally, holding a mudra in meditation for fifteen minutes a day for two weeks can allow you to start noticing the benefits in everyday life. The meditation alone can help lower blood pressure and increase your sense of inner calm and presence in the moment.

If you have never meditated before or if you are out of practice, you may not be able to sit in quiet meditation for fifteen minutes, much less hold a mudra for that time. To build up to the recommended practice, try a five-minute session. Set a timer, hopefully with a pleasant chime, to go off at the appointed time so that you won't be watching the clock. When your meditation begins, you have two choices: you can sit in silent, receptive meditation, or you can set an intention to focus upon.

When performing silent, receptive meditation, the goal is to clear your mind and allow the mudra to be like an antenna for receiving messages from spirit. You will find it much tougher to clear your mind than to focus on something. Try first to focus on your breathing. If you want to set an intention to focus upon, choose one before sitting down to meditate. As you form the mudra, imagine that you are molding the universe into your intention with your hands. During meditation, when your mind wanders from your intention, simply breathe deeply and bring your focus back. Over time and with practice, you will be able to hold your intention for longer periods of time.

Lesser Mudra Practice

The Greater and Lesser Mudra Practices are helpful for holding your awareness on mudras for extended periods of time. These meditations can be done before you have mastered all the mudras, since the hand positions are quite simple. Rather, the challenge in these Greater and Lesser Mudra Practices is in holding your focus on your hands for longer periods of time.

The Lesser Mudra Practice is done by holding both hands in suchi, which you'll recall is simply holding up the pointer fingers. Take a deep breath and hold your hands together so that the tips of each of your index fingers are just barely touching. The trick to the Lesser Mudra Practice is to hold the point of contact as lightly as humanly possible while still connecting the fingers with touch. You can start by holding your hands apart and then bringing them together so that they only just brush each other. If you have issues with neuropathy or any other insensitivity to touch, you can begin this meditation by pressing your fingers together firmly and then lightening the touch gradually until they are touching as lightly as is possible for you. For an advanced version of this practice, remember to keep your elbows up to your sides and your hands in front of your chest without touching your chest.

During the Lesser Mudra Practice, focus your attention entirely on the touch point between your two fingers. Whenever your attention moves elsewhere, consciously bring your focus back to your hands and to the light point of pressure between them. Since the Lesser Mudra Practice is challenging to the mind and body, it allows you to reaffirm your attention to the mudra with each breath, which trains your mind and body for powerful energy work. At the touch point between your fingers, you may sense a buildup of spiritual energy. Some may feel a tactile sensation such as heat, cold, or a sensation that is prickly or fuzzy or that feels like a pressure different from the ones their own hands can exert on each other. Some people do not sense energy in a tactile way and instead "see" the energy in their mind's eye as a light, color, or other imagery. Still others may simply sense the energy as an inner sense of knowing that it is there. However you do or do not sense the energy during the meditation, know that your ability to sense energy will grow with practice. Perform the Lesser Mudra Practice for ten to fifteen minutes a day for two weeks. If you cannot hold your attention for ten minutes, go back to practicing your meditation basics and expand the length of time that you can spend meditating before beginning your Lesser Mudra Practice. Make sure that you have mastered the Lesser Mudra Practice before moving on to the Greater Mudra Practice.

Greater Mudra Practice

The Greater Mudra Practice is the same concept as the Lesser Mudra Practice, except that you use the trishira mudra, which you will recall is simply tenting all your fingers and the thumbs of your hands so that they each touch at the tips. You may find that it is exponentially harder to focus on the points of contact between all five fingers on both hands than it is to keep your attention on just your index fingers. As with the lesser practice, start by holding your hands apart and then bring them together until the fingertips just barely touch at the lightest pressure that you can maintain. Spend ten to fifteen minutes in meditation for two weeks using the Greater Mudra Practice.

You can learn a lot about yourself by noticing which of your fingers are most difficult to maintain in the lightest connection possible and which fingers come more easily to you. Your pinkie fingers are your Mercury fingers, and they represent your powers of communication, your health, and your ability to make good business deals. Your ring fingers are your Apollo fingers and represent your relationship with fame and attention. Your middle fingers are your Saturn fingers and represent the energies in your life that have to do with duty, obligation, hard work, and father figures. Your index fingers represent your leadership energy and ability as well as your sense of direction in life. Your thumbs are associated with the goddess Rhea and the planet Earth and represent your willpower. Indeed, the Greater Mudra Practice can increase willpower over time.

Labyrinthine Hand for Problem-Solving Meditation

A labyrinth is like a maze, but one in which you cannot get lost. As a meditative tool, a labyrinth can be large enough to move through in a walking meditation or small enough to trace with a pencil on a piece of paper. The purpose of the labyrinth is to go deep into meditation through tracing one's movements through the labyrinth. Some labyrinths are designed to spiral inward, symbolizing the process of going deep into one's mind. After reaching the center of the labyrinth, the person returns by retracing one's steps. Spiritually, one can take a problem into the labyrinth, expecting that it will be either shed or transformed by the time one emerges from the meditation. With this labyrinthine hand meditation, you carry a labyrinth around with you wherever you go, ready to allow you to take any problem into meditation.

Basic silent, receptive meditation involves clearing the mind of all thought. It is quite difficult to clear one's mind of thought, so focusing on one's breathing is a shortcut to living in the here and now. In more advanced meditation, breath control can be part of achieving a trance state. This labyrinthine hand exercise is meant to allow you to draw attention and spiritual energy to your hands while simultaneously remaining aware of your breathing. For the beginning meditator, keeping this split focus between hands and breath can feel impossible, so be gentle with yourself if you notice your attention jumping back and forth. Simply notice when your thoughts become unfocused and renew your attempts.

Begin by holding one hand in front of you with fingers spread. With your other hand, you will be tracing the outline of the first hand. Begin at the base of the thumb. As you inhale, draw your finger slowly up your thumb to its tip. As you exhale, continue tracing your finger down into the webbing between your thumb and index finger. By the time you have finished tracing the hand one way, you will have taken five breaths. Reverse the path and retrace your movements to take five more breaths. Now, switch hands and repeat the pattern both times again for a total of twenty breaths for the entire exercise.

Breathe and Connect with Your Soul

Many meditations, like the previous ones, involve focusing on your breathing. Here are some benefits for such breath focus:

First, paying attention to your breath becomes a good focal point. Yes, to simply focus on breathing in meditation may sound like a beginner's way of doing things, but it is, in fact, an advanced form of meditation. Second, having a focus is much easier than eliminating all thought. If you must choose one focus, the best focus is your breathing. Third, attending to your breathing anchors you both to the present moment and to your physical body. Without any further effort, you've just achieved a spiritual centering by simply turning your awareness toward your breath. The earlier meditations used your natural breathing rhythm, but the following meditation encourages you to explore your ability to control your breathing.

The mudra hamsasya, which is the one made by touching your index finger to your thumb, can represent your soul energy when it is moved up and down your body at the wrist. To make this movement, hold the hand in front of your chest with your pinched fingers up and the back of your hand facing down. Draw your hand down as if you were unzipping a zipper. When you reach your navel, rotate the back of your hand upward to reverse the motion as if you were zipping up a zipper. When you reach the crown of your head, repeat the downward movement. Okay, now that you've got that pattern down, I'd like you to practice matching the movement to your breath. When you breathe in, your hand goes down, and when you breathe out, your hand goes up.

You can perform a breathing meditation by either controlling your breathing or not controlling it. When you begin meditating to connect your soul with hamsasya, I recommend breathing normally just so that you can get a hang of coordinating your hands with your breath. Once you get the hang of it, try some simple breath control techniques to deepen and enhance your meditation practice. Controlling your breathing has two added benefits. First, using your own force of will to control your body will intensify your focus on your breath and help prevent your attention from wandering elsewhere and dissipating some of the benefits of your meditation. Second, slower controlled breath will slow your heart rate and allow you to reap the potential health and stress relief benefits of the resulting calm.

Place your other hand on your chest to feel your heartbeat. You may wonder by now which hand to use for which purpose. It doesn't matter which hand you use to make hamsasya and which hand touches your heart. Ideally, you will be able to do the practice with either hand. You can alternate them to practice. However, some people may find it easier to move hamsasya with the dominant hand, so go ahead and try that first while you're getting started.

Count your heartbeats and try to breathe in for four heartbeats and breathe out for four heartbeats. A more advanced practice is to breathe in for four heartbeats, hold for four heartbeats, breathe out for four heartbeats, and hold for four heartbeats. If you struggle to breathe so slowly and deeply for any reason, don't beat yourself up about it. It's okay to return to breathing normally and sync your hand movements to whatever breathing your body allows. If you do use your heartbeat to match breaths, you'll notice that your breathing and heart rate naturally get slower together and that's a good thing. When you finish this meditation, you should feel relaxed and in tune with your body. Perform this meditation for fifteen minutes, or as long as you are able.

Shield against Bad Vibes

Picture this: You're on a crowded commuter train in a foreign country and a particularly creepy individual stands quite close to you. He's not close enough to pickpocket you, but he's close enough that he is invading your personal space, especially since the vibe that you get from him is negative, as if he's just looking for somebody with whom to pick a fight. There's a simple shield that you can make with the chakram mudra that will extend your natural energetic shield to repel negative energy. This brief meditation can be done in public places and is also useful for creating inner calm if there are too many people around, for example, in a busy and overcrowded supermarket.

Everyone has a natural halo of spiritual energy that surrounds their body. Some people call this an aura. Your aura can be extended for many reasons.

Perhaps you want to perform on stage and be noticed by a talent scout. Perhaps you want to reach out spiritually and connect with someone else. And, in this case, you want to sharpen the edges of that energy and extend it to push out any negativity that you don't want to be near you. For this, you'll need a combination of visualization and a moving mudra. Place your palms together with your fingers at right angles to each other and then rotate your palms against each other so that the directions of your fingers trade places. At the start, one hand will have fingers to the sky and the other will have fingers pointing forward. At the end, the positions of the hands will be reversed. This will make the chakram mudra generate energy.

As you move your hands, see energy surrounding you in your mind's eye. This part can be up to your ability to visualize and how your own natural energy pattern manifests, so it can vary. Some people may see a circle of brightly colored flames surrounding themselves. The flames can be any color at all. Some may see a bubble of energy or some other protective barrier. Visualize the barrier around your body becoming sharper and more intense. If there are colors, the colors become more vibrant. If there is a structure to your shield, it becomes opaque and substantial. The use of the mudra will aid the thickening of your shield, so you may find it becomes a bit larger too, and that's okay. In your mind's eye, see any negativity bouncing off your shield and returning harmlessly to the earth or its sender.

Angry Argument Meditation

Whenever you're having an angry conflict with a loved one, it is prudent to take twenty minutes to calm yourself before continuing the conversation. Otherwise, it's easy to say something that you don't mean and, sadly, might never be forgotten. Also, you may not present your side of the debate as convincingly had your senses and mind not been full of rage. The Angry Argument Meditation comes to the rescue when you must excuse yourself from a conflict and find something to do for those twenty minutes.

Let us say that you're arguing with your partner about whether to make an expensive purchase. You know that it's a bad investment and that you shouldn't be making the purchase right now, but your partner is disagreeing with you, and, before you know it, you can sense that your voices are becoming raised and your argument is becoming clipped and snarky. Take a few deep breaths if you need to, and use the keep it together mudra to allow you to speak the following words as lovingly as possible. Say, "I'm sorry, I can't think or speak properly until I've had a breather. I would like to talk about this some more, but right now I need to take some time to meditate for myself. I will see you in twenty minutes."

Exit the room immediately, as calmly as possible, and find a solitary space in which to meditate. It is time to use this meditation for self-soothing. What you should not do is rehearse the points you want to make in your argument when you return. Set a timer and use these twenty minutes only for the purpose of self-soothing. Just trust that you'll be able to plan more coherently after your meditation. Begin by holding the heart (hridaya) mudra. This can be done one-handed, but I recommend making the pose with both hands. Curl your index finger into the palm of your hand, and touch your thumb to the tips of your middle and ring fingers while allowing your pinkie to extend. You can do this seated cross-legged on the floor or on a cushion with your hands resting on your knees or in any other relaxed position. Relax your shoulders. Relax your forehead. Allow the tongue to drop from the roof of your mouth. Don't forget to breathe.

Keep your focus on your hands. Whenever your attention wanders back to the argument, bring your attention back to your hands. You can use a word like *om* or *peace* to realign your mind to your purpose, or you can practice controlling your breathing by breathing in for four heartbeats and breathing out for four heartbeats. Peace begins from within, so it is important that you have returned to a near-baseline emotional state before moving on to the next mudra. Kilaka is a mudra to help you come to a harmonious accord with your partner. Link your pinkie fingers together with one hand above the other. Hold this mudra in front of your chest without touching your chest, keeping your elbows up but shoulders down. Check in with your body to see if there are any residual points of tension. Keep holding the kilaka mudra until the timer chimes that your meditation is done. Take a deep breath and return to continue the courageous conversation with your partner, knowing that you can repeat this process whenever necessary to take back your power from your angry monkey mind. This meditation is also useful in situations when you keep getting a paranoia or anxiety that a loved one is mad at you even though he or she assures you that there is no animosity held toward you.

Knock Their Socks Off Meditation

This meditation is designed to allow your best self to be put forward. Whether you need to be perceived well by others during a job interview or you're giving a performance to a crowd of cheering spectators, you're going to want your energy and confidence to stay consistently high. Designed as a series of three meditations that can be run through fairly quickly while in a waiting room before an interview or performance, this meditation begins during rehearsal or in preparation for the big day. Perform the series of mudras in a longer meditation after each time you practice or prepare or after dressing up for the big moment. Aim for about ten minutes. The purpose of these longer meditations is to anchor the mudras in your mind during times when you feel calm and prepared. That way, when you briefly run through them in the waiting room or backstage while the pressure is on, your subconscious will snap back into the state of mind in which you feel ready to do your best.

Begin with the empowerment mudra by pressing the middle and ring fingers together at the second knuckles and tenting your pinkie, index fingers, and thumbs. The purpose of the empowerment mudra is to concentrate your personal power in this moment so that you can evoke it later when you want to perform well. Look down and see three triangles formed by your tented pinkies, index fingers, and thumbs, respectively. Gaze at the empowerment mudra for about five minutes. Then, switch to the "yes" mudra by separating your hands and touching the tips of your thumbs to the inside of the first joint of your middle finger on each hand. The purpose of using the "yes" mudra is to help incline the minds of your audience to accept your performance and to give you a positive response. Hold the "yes" mudra until you near the end of your meditation. Finally, perform the moving chakram mudra by placing your palms together with fingers at right angles to each other and rotating them so that they rub together and alternate as if they were turning spokes on a wheel. The chakram mudra is working to expand the reach of your personal energy pattern, making your persona seem larger than life.

After you've practiced this mudra sequence frequently, you can run through the three mudras in under a minute. Use these mudras surreptitiously beneath a table or in your lap. The first two can even be performed behind your back, with the third having all the appearance of dusting off your hands. As you quickly run through the mudras, recall to your mind the feelings you had when you were fully preparing for the present moment.

Creativity Stimulation Meditation

Whether you're an artist or simply trying to think of what on earth you're going to make for dinner, we all need a little inspiration sometimes. This meditation will boost your motivation and help you problem-solve with innovation. Like the previous meditation, this creativity meditation is a series of three mudras. It is suggested that you spend at least five minutes with each pose in meditation. You can use this fifteen-minute meditation anytime you get writer's block or need to brainstorm. If you're working on a larger project that needs sustained innovation on a day-to-day basis, use this meditation daily for at least two weeks.

Begin with the yoni mudra. The yoni represents the seat of creation in the human body, the feminine well of desire and generativity that brings forth all life. You are stirring the cauldron of birth when you use this powerful mudra, so avoid this meditation if you are afraid of becoming pregnant, since literal fertility can go hand in hand with the figurative fertility of a mind abundant with creativity. Hold your hands with fingers loosely spread, palms up, with the pinkie and ring fingers of your dominant hand overlapping the two of your nondominant hand (if you are ambidextrous, use right over left). As you sit in meditation, imagine that all the forces of creation in the universe are being drawn toward your hands.

After five minutes, change to the shivalingam mudra. Bring your nondominant hand to chest level, flat with palm upward. Take your dominant hand in the thumbs-up sign, begin with it floating above your flattened hand,

and move it forward, down, and behind so that it makes a full circle around your flat hand before resting, thumbs-up still, on top of the flattened hand. The masculine, generative force of this mudra will amplify your motivation and will work in concert with the yoni mudra.

Finally, for the last five minutes of your meditation, use padmakosha to evoke these creative forces that you have stirred up within yourself. Hold your hands with palms upward and then push all your fingers and your thumbs up so that your hand appears to be a blooming flower. If you are seated, you can rest your hands on your knees in meditation at this point. Imagine that your hands are both receptive and projective—that is, that they draw in ideas like satellite dishes as you breathe in, and while you breathe out, the creative forces that you've stirred up flow out of you through your arms and radiate outward from the palms of your hands. When you have completed the meditation, turn immediately to your creative project. Don't allow yourself to do any other activity until you've worked on the creative project, even if that means sitting in meditation for a while longer than originally intended.

Healthy Sleep Meditation

Meditation lends itself to healthy sleep, especially if you are the type of person who normally falls asleep during attempts at meditation. If you don't want to fall asleep during meditation, it is advisable to only meditate at a time of the day when your circadian rhythm is in its waking cycle. Reserve this specialized sleep mudra only for times when you want to fall asleep. It is also possible to train yourself to fall asleep when holding the mudra without ruining your ability to meditate without falling asleep when using it for other purposes. Essentially, you are practicing self-hypnosis.

The Healthy Sleep Meditation needs a period of mind training before it will work for occasional use when you need it. Thus, I recommend that you perform this practice even if you normally fall asleep easily. That way, you can have this tool in your back pocket when added stress or excitement makes your usual sleep routine difficult. The training period for this mudra is two weeks for at least twenty minutes. It is normal to take twenty minutes to fall asleep in a period known as sleep latency. The purpose of the training is to set the khattva mudra as an anchor in your mind—that is, to form a powerful association between the mudra and your natural sleep process. That way, you can use the mudra as a key to unlock a specific state of consciousness—in this case, restful sleep.

Ideally, begin working with khattva when you are not having extra pressure or disruption to routine in your life that contraindicates normal sleep. Set yourself up for sleep success by setting reasonable hours of wakefulness, turning off screens an hour before bed, and making sure you get daily exercise. During the time when you are most likely to fall asleep, hold the khattva mudra by folding your thumbs into your palms and touching your middle and ring fingers to each other with both hands to form a bed. Your pinkie and index fingers form the four legs of the bed. Touch your hands together very lightly and focus on the point of contact in the same way that you would for the Greater Mudra Practice and Lesser Mudra Practice. While you hold the mudra, tell yourself that you are about to fall into restful sleep and wake rejuvenated and ready for the day. Ideally, you will hold the mudra lightly until you fall asleep. The more often that you use this mudra to fall asleep, the shorter your sleep latency will become.

There's Too Much Stuff on My Plate Meditation

It is easy to work oneself into a panic upon hitting a point of overwhelm, which then makes it nearly impossible to get started efficiently on whatever work is required. If you have volunteered for too many things or are trying to split your time between work, family, and social life, you may have felt such a sense of being engulfed by responsibilities and losing your sense of self. Do not find yourself giving up and being unproductive. Instead, use this meditation to get yourself back on track and to strike down your obligations one by one. I know that it may seem counterintuitive to spend twenty minutes in meditation when you feel like you don't have enough hours in the day already, but trust me. Streamlining your ability to conquer the right tasks will more than make up for lost time with optimized time. I have organized this meditation in four simple steps so that it won't add any confusion to your stress.

Step 1: Stop what you are doing. If you feel like you cannot stop rushing around in a panic, add the keep it together mudra as step number zero. Once you have found yourself a peaceful spot for the next twenty minutes, form the atman mudra by touching your middle fingers together at the first knuckle and touching the rest of your fingers and your thumbs together at the tips. Spend at least five minutes holding atman while you ask yourself this important question: "Which of the tasks ahead of me align with my true self?" The purpose of this question is to set yourself some priorities. The tasks that best lead you to your true self will emerge as the most important, while those that are inauthentic or can be delegated to other people will filter through your thought process as lower priorities.

Step 2: Once you have prioritized the tasks on your plate, we will paradoxically first turn our attention to those tasks that are low priority right now. Form the "no" mudra by touching your index finger to your thumb with each hand and then linking the two hands together as if a chain, allowing the remaining fingers to tent and touch. Hold this "no" mudra briefly while speaking out loud the tasks that are low priority.

Step 3: Form samputa with your hands by cupping them together as if you were holding a captured butterfly and briefly visualize putting all the low-priority tasks into a box formed by your hands. You can now, in your mind's eye, place the box somewhere for safekeeping.

Step 4: Form the body integration mudra by folding your fingers into your palms, touching your fists together at the second and last knuckles, and then allowing your thumbs to touch at the pads. While you hold this meditation for the remainder of your meditation's duration, bring back to the forefront of your mind the highest-priority task that you must complete. Visualize yourself completing the very first step of the most important task. At the end of your meditation, immediately get up and get to work on this high-priority item until you have at least completed the first step that you have visualized.

Love Blooms Meditation

The purpose of this meditation is to draw a soul mate into your life, whether romantic or platonic in nature. A soul mate, in this sense, is somebody with whom you share a connection on an intimate level, as if your energies vibrate on the same frequency. We're talking about a person in your life with whom you can share perfect love and perfect trust. This soul mate will feel close to you even when time and space keep you apart. Best of all, the soul mate attracted by this meditation will love you for who you truly are.

If you struggle with self-care and self-love, this meditation can be very healthy for you, but it may also be quite challenging. If you struggle with a lot of personal demons and feel too disingenuous when trying this meditation, check out the "Samputa Shadow Work" section on page 190. Shadow work is the process of coming to terms with your darker aspects and integrating them into your sense of self to combat self-loathing.

The sequence of five mudras used in this meditation blends smoothly together to imitate the blooming of a flower. You may have noticed that many mudras can be made to appear like blooming flowers, which makes using them an excellent way to symbolically show beautiful ideas becoming physical manifestation. This meditation is challenging, but it also teaches you how to use these mudras in a cycle so that you can add this movement to other rituals. Symbolically, this meditation represents combining joy and trust in yourself to offer the best and truest version of yourself to the universe asking for love. In order, the mudras are: bliss, trust, empowerment, soul vibration, and pushpaputa. Reminders for these mudras will be listed on page 99 as a recipe for this moving meditation, but do take the time to focus on the application of the following meanings behind the mudras. To illustrate this exercise without becoming tedious, here's a short story about a woman hoping for her future husband.

On the far side of a city full of skyscrapers, Jeanette awoke well after sunrise one lazy Saturday morning. While brushing her teeth, she gazed into the mirror at herself. She had only just switched on the coffee pot and the first cup would be ready by the time she had completed her five-minute morning meditation, a devotional to herself. As a yoga practitioner might use the sun salutation, Jeanette had been starting her day with this meditation for a couple of weeks, and she was considering continuing the practice. She seated herself on some thrift store cushions that had been placed carefully in a bay window breakfast nook that she had set aside for prayer, meditation, and journaling.

Using her hands to form the bliss mudra, Jeanette began with a focus on self-love, trying to reach deep for her feelings of compassion and peace. Index fingers connected at the first knuckle as if forming a heart with the tented thumbs, Jeanette's other fingers connected at the second knuckle. When she felt secure in that feeling within her, she shifted her hands by just moving her index fingers to tent opposite her thumbs to form the trust mudra. Jeanette allowed her feelings to shift to a trust in her own judgement of people and in her hope to find trustworthy kindred spirits in the world. Having lived enough life to have trust shaken in people, Jeanette spent a few extra moments reassuring herself that, even if she didn't have perfect trust in many people now, she deserved trustworthy people in her life.

Next, Jeanette shifted the mudra again, this time simply by moving her pinkie fingers to tent along with the index fingers. Her other fingers remained connected to each other at the second knuckles. This is the empowerment mudra, and Jeanette allowed herself to feel empowered to find and share love and trust. Deep in her heart, Jeanette was certain that she was worthy of adoration. Moving her hands to the soul vibration mudra simply meant parting her hands slightly so that her middle and ring fingers connected at the first knuckles instead of the second. Jeanette allowed her own energy signature to amplify, as if her soul shone bright like a beacon. Allowing her mind's eye to roam, Jeanette visualized her own energy like a ball of yellow light that surrounded her body, radiating from her belly to fill the room with a bright glow.

Sustaining the beautiful image of her shimmering aura in her mind, Jeanette released the mudra and cupped her hands into pushpaputa, slowly raising her arms as if in offering to the sky that she could see in her window through her lightly parted eyelids. More quickly, Jeanette ran through the sequence of mudras two more times to cement them in her memory for next time. She smelled coffee in the air. With her act of self-care complete and a sense of acceptance wrapping her like a warm hug, Jeanette was ready to start her day. Here's a cheat sheet of the meditation.

1. Bliss: Index fingers connected at first knuckle. Other fingers at second knuckle. Thumbs at tips.
2. Trust: Index fingers unfold to tent at the tips. Other fingers still at second knuckle.
3. Empowerment: Pinkie fingers unfold to tent. Middle and ring fingers still at second knuckle.
4. Soul Vibration: Pull the hands gently so that middle and ring fingers connect at first knuckle.
5. Pushpaputa: Open hands to cup them together like a bowl.

One quick word about the efficacy of love spells since this meditation resembles one. The mode of action of this Love Blooms Meditation is focused on self-love and being able to radiate your best self into the universe, thus attracting people to you who share your vibration. It is important not to try to force a specific person to love you, especially with this meditation, since it can backfire. If the person you're crushing on is the right person for you, the energy and attitude given to you by this meditation should be magnetic to them anyway. If you try to focus on an individual during this meditation, rather than making them fall in love with you, it will instead imprint their energies onto you. This could cause you to become blindly devoted, just as a baby duck imprints on the first adult duck it sees. It's philosophically debatable whether a devoted one should imprint his or her energies on a beloved, but here I'd like to argue to err on the side of boundaries and personal autonomy, since this is about attracting a new love rather than sealing a consensual marriage. Instead, focus on improving yourself, and an improved love life and friendships will naturally follow.

Note that relationships are hard work, and this meditation won't necessarily make the love of your life fall into your lap. It can take years of work on yourself before you feel worthy enough of love to relax into a healthy relationship. However, you don't have to be perfect to powerfully draw loving energy to yourself. In fact, the gentle and loving nature of this meditation makes it ideal for practice by the brokenhearted, even if you do not yet feel ready for a new relationship. The nature of meditating on self-love means that you are also protecting your heart and your sense of self until you are ready to fully give your heart to another. No matter how imperfect or broken you feel you are, you are already deserving of love. This meditation can help you achieve it.

Building and Extending Your Meditation Practice

Note that any of the preceding meditations, except the Angry Argument Meditation, can be used with a partner in addition to solo. Whether you're teaching a meditation class or simply connecting with a spouse or child, you can mirror each other's mudras. Another option for partnered meditation is for one of the pair to hold a receptive mudra while the other holds an active mudra. One partner can also hold a feminine mudra while the other holds a masculine mudra, regardless of the genders of the meditation participants. More about specific partnered meditations can be found in the next section.

Hopefully, some of the meditations in this chapter will inspire you to practice meditation with some regularity. The techniques can be simplified or shortened if they seem too difficult or impractical for you at this point in your life. Remember that meditation, in its simplest form, is the ability to ride just one breath from its beginning to its conclusion, and then perhaps another and another. If you can only meditate for one breath, do so and hold a mudra to boost the power of that meditation's intention. This is the beauty of a mudra. Your hands act like antennae to amplify your power out into the world or to receive power from divine sources.

I know that meditation does not often feel glamorous or exciting, since it involves a lot of sitting still and the challenging prospect of controlling your own mind. But the truth is, all the power of magic in the world stems from your ability to hold complete dominion over your own mind. One would struggle to master more advanced magical and spiritual concepts without first having a working ability to meditate. This meditation chapter may thus be the most difficult chapter in this book.

Choose the most motivating meditation in this chapter to practice on a regular basis and schedule that meditation time in your calendar, even if you'll be using a minute of it until you build up your stamina for longer periods of meditation. Once you can meditate for a full fifteen minutes or more, strive to keep meditation time in your schedule. Some days you may feel like you need meditation more than others, but keeping the discipline to meditate when your mindset is not naturally gravitating that way is how you will gain additional power. Treat your meditation practice as a valuable spiritual discipline. Over time, you may notice additional health benefits and reduced stress that spring naturally from regular meditation.

Partnered Mudras

Most of the meditations in chapter 2 can be used with a partner, but there are some specific meditations that work better with a kindred spirit. Sharing your spirituality with a romantic partner, a best friend, or a family member can be an excellent way to bond with each other. You will also have an accountability buddy if you want to make partnered meditation a regular practice. Both of you will enjoy the benefits of meditation, such as lower blood pressure and improved mood. Before we launch into some examples of partnered meditations, here are some of the building blocks that make partnered meditations effective. As with solo meditation, the basic principles of meditation apply, such as minimizing distractions and gradually increasing your meditation stamina until you can meditate for at least twenty continuous minutes a day. With a partner, that means keeping the meditation as short as both people can comfortably tolerate and letting the person with less stamina take the lead when increasing session duration. Partnered meditation might increase the need for grounding after meditation as well. Beginners can get over-enthusiastic about projecting their energy and feel depleted. Consider psychic vampires (see page 157 for more information). Beginners in partnered meditations might accidentally make some of the same mistakes psychic vampires do in their eagerness to receive energy.

Secret Handshakes: Best friends and secret societies alike often share a secret handshake greeting. Using physical contact between two people forming the same mudra amplifies its effect, and when physical contact connects two different mudras, it can combine their effects, creating a combined mudra that cannot exist in solo meditation. A simple way to use the secret handshake method is to simply rest your hands atop your partner's hands or vice versa.

Mirroring: Humans are wired to copy each other, which is why a baby copies a smile and a wave from even a stranger. When using mudras to mirror, this technique can create a powerful connection when one partner takes the lead and slowly changes one mudra into another mudra while the other person copies his or her slow movements.

Sending and Receiving: Some mudras are active or projective, meaning that they move energy and can send it to other people, places, or planes of existence. Other mudras are passive and receptive, meaning they help people detect spiritual energy by acting as a conduit, and assist in the process of integrating spiritual energy into your being. When one partner holds a passive mudra while the other holds an active mudra, an energy exchange begins.

Trust and Soul Vibration

Our first partnered meditation example is one that makes use of sending and receiving energy. The purpose of the Trust and Soul Vibration Meditation is to connect your authentic self with a partner in order to establish deeper trust between the two of you. Suitable for either romantic or platonic partnerships, consider doing this meditation with your soul mate, your best friend, or a close family member. Using the Trust and Soul Vibration Meditation can help solidify your bond after it is shaken by a perceived betrayal. For example, imagine a sister who became alarmed when her brother mentioned suicidal thoughts and immediately called the police for a wellness check. Her brother knows that his sister's intentions were good and pure, but he felt a sense of shock that she went behind his back to call the police. If the siblings did this meditation together, the brother may have an easier time forgiving the sister for doing what she had to do, and the sister may feel more connected with her brother during an emotionally difficult time.

The soul vibration mudra will be the projective mudra in this meditation, and the trust mudra will be the receptive mudra. Each partner will take turns with each mudra. It is best for the one who feels the most betrayed to do the trust vibration last, so in the example above, the brother would form the soul vibration mudra first and the sister would take on the trust mudra. After a few minutes, the two would switch. The amount of time should be as long as both can tolerate, with a goal of up to twenty minutes for each. If one participant is new to meditation, take care to make the meditation short enough to be comfortable, even if it is as little as thirty seconds each.

The soul vibration mudra is formed by touching the first knuckle of your last three fingers while touching the tips of your index fingers and the tips of your thumbs. The trust mudra is identical to the soul vibration mudra, except your last three fingers connect at the second knuckle instead of the first. After the meditation, discuss with your partner how you feel. It may be important for one or both of you to ground yourselves if you feel jitters, dizziness, brain fog, or fatigue. Meditations in this section should generally leave you feeling refreshed and clear-headed, but any partnered meditation involving an exchange of energy can end up feeling a little imbalanced for beginning practitioners. Nothing that cannot be fixed with a bit of grounding. With experience, you and your partner will feel only positive energy and clarity from partnered meditations.

Coming of Age

In Western culture, we don't have very many ceremonies to celebrate a girl becoming a woman or a boy becoming a man. Other cultures, however, have celebrations and even challenges to mark the milestone of reaching adulthood, and such practices may actually be helpful for the young adult to gain confidence and a sense of becoming a peer with respected adults in the community. In many cultures, these ceremonies are gender specific since there are particular gendered roles within the culture and community. In this meditation I will use some gendered examples but also one that is not gender specific in order to include those who, for any reason, do not identify with the gendered rituals. Each meditation will make use of the mirroring concept of partnered mudra meditation.

In the examples that follow, I will write as if they are being done with a parent and child, for example a father and son or a mother and daughter. However, please feel free to substitute any maternal figure in the youth's life for a mother and any paternal figure in the youth's life for a father. Sometimes our spiritual parental figures can be more meaningful than problematic biological ones, and I recognize and support that.

For Women

The two partners should sit face-to-face. Begin the meditation with each partner forming the empowerment mudra by pressing the second knuckles of her middle and ring fingers together, while allowing index fingers and pinkie fingers to tent and touch tips. This is a time to reflect with each other on how much growth has occurred in the young adult. The mother should gaze at the daughter's mudra and the daughter should gaze at the mother's mudra. Both partners should focus on how womanhood can be empowering.

Gradually, the mother should slowly change her mudra to the sign of the Goddess with both hands. This can be done gracefully by slowly pulling the hands apart and, with each hand, curving the index finger and thumb to make a crescent moon, allowing the remaining fingers to curl up completely and tuck into the palm. She should then cross hands at the wrist to symbolize both the waxing and the waning moon. The two crescent moons, with the mother in the middle, represent the triple moon that symbolizes three phases of a woman's life: maiden, mother, and crone. The trick is to make this mudra shift as slowly as possible. Meanwhile, the daughter should mirror the change in mudras by focusing on copying her mother's movements. The energy between the two women will intensify as they focus on each other's mudras and the slow movements. When both women share the sign of the Goddess mudras with hands crossed, they should remain in meditation for as long as is practical given the stamina of the least experienced meditator. This meditation should be brief, gentle, and celebratory.

For Men

The two partners should sit face-to-face. Begin the meditation with each partner forming the body integration mudra by holding the hands together at the third knuckles with fingers folded flat against the palms and thumbs touching at the tips. This is the time to reflect on how the young adult has been shaping his body, mind, and spirit with his actions. The father should slowly change the mudra into the shivalingam mudra. Initiate the change by pulling the hands apart and unrolling your left hand into a flat platform. Your right hand then takes on the "thumbs-up" sign and moves first in front of the left hand, then circles down and behind the hand near your chest to end by planting the right hand firmly on the left hand's palm. At this point, the focus is on visualizing the type of man the young adult has become and will continue to grow to be. The pair should remain in meditation for as long as is practical given the stamina of the least experienced meditator. Remember, this is not a staring contest.

For Neutral or Other Genders

This gender-neutral meditation can be used for situations in which the man-to-man or woman-to-woman scenario does not apply, or if this version is simply preferable. As the meditation begins, the two partners should face each other and both form the inner vision mudra by interlacing the knuckles of the pointer and middle fingers, right over left, and then touching the thumbs together. Take time to reflect openly about the young adult's inner vision of self and how that has formed the young adult taking part in this meditation today.

With each partner focusing on the other's mudra, the parental figure should slowly change the inner vision mudra into the self-acceptance mudra. To make the change fluidly, push the palms together into prayer pose (anjali mudra) and then curl the finger of your right hand over the curled finger of your left hand to frame the thumbs. The parent should focus on expressing acceptance of the young adult, while the youth reflects on the journey to acceptance of the new adult body, mind, and spirit. The pair should remain in meditation for as long as is practical given the stamina of the least experienced meditator. Be gentle and joyful as you celebrate growth and the courage to change.

Upon Waking

A morning ritual can help you reconnect with your partner or each family member as you jump-start your day with positive energy. This morning meditation uses the secret handshake method of partnered mudra work. Stretching your hands and using physical touch to connect with a loved one or two is an excellent way to boost the happy brain chemicals that help you have a good attitude. After all, there are no bad days, just bad attitudes. It is a great idea to meditate in the morning before you look at your phone or your computer or any other screens, before you answer important work or school messages, and before you look at the news of the day. This brief, less-than-five-minute, meditation can fit into nearly any busy morning.

Step 1: Begin with one partner, whoever wants to initiate the meditation, extending a hand in alapadma mudra. That is, the hand will be extended forward with palm up, fingers splayed but pinkie pointed skyward so that the fingers form the appearance of a flower blossom. The other partner should hold their hand in hamsasya or the prana mudra, which looks like the OK sign, and touch the connected tips of the index finger and thumb to the center of the palm of the other partner holding alapadma, as if it is a bee visiting the flower. The energy of these mudras helps you start your day with the flow of renewed and enhanced spiritual energy.

Step 2: Next, the two of you will share the empowerment mudra. Each of you will form one of the hands required to make the whole mudra. Sharing a mudra is easier than it sounds. To make the empowerment mudra, both of you simply form the "I love you" hand sign in American Sign Language.

One partner holds up his or her left hand and the other partner holds up his or her right hand. To make the "I love you" sign in ASL, face your palm toward your partner and fold down your middle and ring fingers so that the thumb, index finger, and pinkie finger are the remaining fingers pointing up. Now, touch your hands together. The folded fingers will naturally rest against each other, and the tips of each of your corresponding fingers and thumbs will touch. You two have made the empowerment mudra. Hold the mudra together and meditate on channeling this positive energy of shared connection toward everything you do this day. Take at least nine deep breaths with your eyes closed. When you are finished, open your eyes and wait for your partner, if necessary, to finish.

Upon Going to Bed

A bedtime meditation is a silent prayer for good health. This partnered meditation can be done with a bedmate or a family member before bed to invoke pleasant dreams and revitalizing sleep. This meditation harnesses the power of the secret handshake technique and the sending and receiving method, this time back-to-back. This exercise makes use of three mudras. If you are doing this meditation with more than one person, like a family, switch all three mudras to the mirroring technique and have one family member lead the rest through all three mudras.

Step 1: Begin the bedtime meditation with the shankha (or conch) mudra. One partner extends the left hand and the other partner grips his or her thumb. When the person initiating the handshake wraps his or her fingers around the partner's hand that grips the thumb, it completes the shared shankha mudra. This mudra has a calming effect and symbolizes calling each other to bed. Decide which one of you will begin with the inner vision mudra and which one of you will begin with the prana integration mudra. This shankha stage of the meditation is brief, but now the real meat of the meditation will begin.

Step 2: Partners should sit back-to-back with eyes closed. Having already agreed in step 1 which person will perform which mudra, one partner begins with the prana integration mudra in order to invite balance into both partners' lives. The prana mudra integrates spiritual energy into the physical body, helping you feel soothed, ready for healing, and grounded. To make the prana integration mudra, fold your hands together with interlaced fingers, and focus on the feeling of peacefulness.

The other partner starts with the inner vision mudra by interlacing the knuckles of the pointer and middle fingers, right over left, and then touching the thumbs together. Dreams will be summoned by this use of the inner vision mudra coupled with the body integration mudra. With eyes closed, one or both partners may see visions at this time in the mind's eye, and that is okay. Before switching mudras, the partners should hold these poses for at least nine breaths.

Step 3: When each partner is finished with breathing into the inner vision or prana integration mudra, he or she should hold arms slightly out to the side with hands drooped in dola mudra to signify the readiness to switch mudras. Dola is another calming and grounding mudra. When both partners are displaying dola mudra, switch so that the first partner is now doing the inner vision mudra and the second is practicing the prana integration mudra. Hold for at least nine deep breaths or until one partner is snoring, whichever happens first.

Parting Ways

Here is a meditation to say goodbye. The parting ways meditation is not designed for a brief and temporary goodbye. For those "see you tomorrow" moments I still recommend a hug. After the COVID-19 pandemic of 2020, I made a promise to myself to never forget the power of hugging a friend goodbye. But some goodbyes are more meaningful than others. For the exchange student heading home, the college student moving to a dorm room, or a farewell to a loved one who may be leaving your life indefinitely, a hug may not seem enough. This meditation makes use of the sending and receiving method. Since so many cultures say goodbye with a gift, it only seems fitting that we should be conscious of the energetic gifts we give to those who encounter us in life.

The two mudras used for this goodbye are kilaka and the triangle of manifestation mudra. Kilaka is a two-handed mudra that you make by linking your pinkie fingers together with one hand directly above the other. The person who is radiating the energy of the kilaka mudra should focus on joyful memories of the time spent together. The kilaka mudra enhances your peaceful and friendly vibrations, which can help if the parting is bittersweet. The other partner should hold the triangle of manifestation mudra by forming a triangle by touching the index fingers together and the thumbs together. This partner should gaze through the triangle at the kilaka mudra that is being held. Both will radiate the intentions to go forward from this parting of ways while holding the joyful memories shared and radiating that joy from within.

~3~
Mudras in Your Spiritual Practice

In shows and video games, a sorceress or wizard always casts a spell with a flourish. In real life, magic is often quite a bit less theatrical. Magic is the art and science of altering your world to match your inner need. Real magic can be done while sitting in subdued meditation with no movement at all. All the action is going on inside the mind through visualization and fervent focus of emotion and desire. However, you can accentuate this focus and direction of your own personal spiritual energy with mudras. Energy, in this context, is the universal life force that can be used for manifestation. Martial artists and energy healers have known for centuries that energy can be directed with the hands. Modern magic can in practice be as theatrical as you choose, even if sparks really don't fly out of your hands except in your mind's eye. In this chapter, you'll learn many different practical applications of gestures to make everyday acts like lighting a candle into graceful spiritual arts. But first, you'll need to learn a little bit about the context of mudras in ritual and the basis for how they work so that you can maximize their performance. Rituals don't have to be something out of a witch's cookbook. Secular life has plenty of rituals, such as weddings and graduations, that can be embellished and enriched with mudras.

Mudras as Worship and Sacred Acts

You've got all the mudras down pat and you're ready to introduce them into some exercises to really manifest your dreams. This is done through ritual. A ritual is an exercise that is done to produce a specific result, usually to get the practitioner into the right headspace to celebrate, give gratitude and love to the universe, or make their hopes and wishes happen. Rituals can be religious or secular, complex or simple. When we do a very complex ritual to create magic, like drawing complicated shapes with our hands, using lots of props, moving around the space, and chanting many words, we call that "high magic." High magic rituals always have a beginning, a middle, and an end. When the ritual is as simple as stirring your coffee a specific way or making a sign over your bed to ward away bad dreams, we call that "low magic." Low magic is often flexible and casual. Another special ritual context that we'll explore at the end of this chapter is ritual storytelling. Storytelling has been used since ancient times to share sacred myths and teach spiritual lessons. Mudras can be a great way to get into character when dramatically retelling a story. Ritual storytelling is usually used in a group context.

Charging Your Mudras to Create the Keys to Your Consciousness

Before you can use mudras for magic, the mudras have to mean something to you. That's why I introduced the meditation chapter before this ritual chapter, so that you could get comfortable with some of the mudras and how they make you feel. The more often they make you feel a specific way after sitting with them for a long time, the more quickly you will slip into that feeling as soon as you form the mudra with your hands on future occasions.

Let me give you a different example of how this works. Have you ever accidentally taken the wrong exit on the highway because you were on "autopilot"? Maybe you were heading to the store and you meant to drive right past the exit to your home, but you were so focused on the road and driving that you exited the highway as if to go home. In this case, you probably shook your head for being so absent-minded and turned around to get back on the highway to continue on to the store. In this example, the highway exit to your home triggered your subconscious because you had used that exit to go home so many times before. This accident is more likely to happen if you were driving during a time when you normally head home. You were in the "going home" headspace after work even though you meant to go to the store, so your hands turned the steering wheel in concert with your subconscious.

In this chapter, you will purposely create triggers for your subconscious that work in concert with your hands. These triggers act like keys to unlock feelings, just like seeing the exit on the highway unlocked the "going home" feeling in your subconscious. Using mudras in this way is nothing new, and they are used in modern practices such as hypnotism and neurolinguistic programming (NLP). So, before you can spice up your everyday life and rituals with mudras to create magic, you have to program them to make them into keys that will trigger the right states of consciousness in a process we call "charging" them. Every time you meditate with a mudra you are charging it, just like every day you drive the same route home from work you're training your subconscious. For the most effective charging, you will need to intensely experience the feeling that you wish to imprint upon the mudra. For this reason, it's important to be aware of your current headspace. If you're having a really frustrating day filled with anger, it's probably not the right time to start working on charging a mudra for peace and harmony, though it would be the perfect time to use that mudra as a tool if you had already charged it over hundreds of meditation sessions.

Charging the Bliss Mudra

Charging mudras looks an awful lot like meditation because it is a type of meditation, so I'll just include one example here: using the bliss mudra for worship to access spirit's life-affirming qualities. The bliss mudra is a perfect choice for a first mudra to charge because it can be used in so many different magical contexts, from high magic to low magic. You can hold the bliss mudra as part of a bigger ritual for a wedding ceremony, or you can quickly use the mudra to mentally go to your happy place when you're feeling stressed or under the weather. In the last chapter, our meditations usually started with forming the mudra and allowing any feelings or senses to come to you through the mudra and the meditation. For charging a mudra, we're going to do things backward. We will start with an intense feeling and then form the mudra to lock the emotion into the mudra.

To get started, choose a day on which you feel generally happy or at least are in a neutral headspace. Make sure that you will not be disturbed for the duration of your meditation, ideally at least twenty minutes to an hour, but you can choose whatever length your current ability to meditate allows. I recommend doing this meditation lying down with your eyes closed. Begin by searching your memory for a time in your life when you felt completely fulfilled and whole as a person, complete bliss, happy and safe. Depending on how life has been going recently, you might have to reach back in your memory for years or even to childhood.

Mentally take yourself back to that place and time and recreate as many of the senses as possible. What were you hearing during that time? What did it smell like? What sensations were you feeling on your skin? "Look" around with your mind's eye and see everything that was present at that location. Open yourself up and allow yourself to feel that emotion again completely until you can't help smiling. Now is the time to form the bliss mudra. Form a heart with your hands, touching thumbs at the tips and curling the index fingers to touch at the first knuckles. Allow your remaining fingers to touch at the second knuckles. Hold the feeling and the mudra for as long as possible. When you have finished, release the mudra. Know that you can hold that mudra at any time to trigger your brain to make that feeling come flooding back. Repetition helps any ritual key work quickly and more effectively. When you repeat this meditation, you may not have to do it as long since it won't take as much work to dig up the memory and the emotion. Repeat the meditation for at least five to fifteen minutes for at least two weeks to solidify it in your mind. Now you have a tool in your Batman tool belt that you can bust out during any ritual to manifest bliss in your life. You can do this with any and all of the mudras on any and all of your emotional states. If a mudra doesn't exist yet for the mental state you want to create, invent one!

Gestures for Manipulating Magical Energy

Holding and meditating on a mudra is not the only thing we can do. We can also use ritual gestures as a physical representation of moving that spiritual energy that can make your dreams come true. The gestures used in this book are based upon the mudras and often move the mudra through space or gradually shift one mudra to another. Some ritual gestures work because they have been used in so many rituals by so many people for so long that the mudra gets added to the collective subconscious. Think of it as if we all had the same highway exit home, except in this case we're all unlocking the same feelings because we all share the same human condition and the same brain structure and the same universal history. You might find that some common ritual gestures don't seem to need charging because you've already charged their component mudras or because they seem to work already due to this phenomenon of the collective subconscious. Let's get started by introducing some building blocks for rituals, and then you'll be given some complete rituals that you can take for a spin.

Invoking Universal Spirit

In many faith traditions, invoking the divine is an important component of worship. You can invoke the divine before prayer or simply to offer gratitude for this wonderful world in which we live. You'll recognize the tripataka mudra from depictions of Hindu deities because they are using it to bless the viewer. You too can bless the world with tripataka. Your inner power is believed to move energy through vortexes of your own personal energy that exist in the palms of your hands, among other places on your body. To invoke your energy, use your index finger to draw a counterclockwise circle on each palm. While you do so, visualize "opening" up this powerful energetic source. Then, form tripataka by holding your palms up, bent at the wrist, flat in pataka, and then folding your ring fingers over at a 90-degree angle to project your blessing out to the world. Now you truly look like a representation of the divine.

Sign for Unity, Balance, Completion

Before starting a ritual, we often create sacred space. You don't have to build a physical temple, because you can create sacred space anywhere you go. One tradition is to salute and invite sacred energies from all four compass points in a practice known as "calling the quarters." The sacred space is often defined by walking or mentally drawing a large circle with an imaginary boundary, which we call "casting the circle." There exists a generic gesture that can be used for calling the quarters during the process of casting a circle to create a magical boundary of protection and containment. To make this gesture, turn your palms outward and gather energy from around you while you bring your hands in toward your chest to blend the external energies with those from your heart chakra, an energetic vortex that colors the energy with your personal power. You can linger a moment, moving your hands around this ball of energy, or you can move straight to thrusting your hands outward with fingertips up and palms out. This gesture can be done once to bless with unity, twice to bless with balance, and three times to seal a spell or ritual moment. When done three times, this building block for ritual is a powerful tool for receiving and sending spiritual energy. Use it to mark poignant moments or to summon what you want and need from any corner of the world. An alternative ritual practice that serves the same function is to draw a pentagram, a five-pointed star, in the air with your finger, but I will save the pentagram drawing examples for the Lesser Banishing Ritual of the Pentagram later in this chapter.

Sign for Drawing Blessings

We could all use a little blessing from spirit sometimes. To bless yourself with divine energy, hold your hands relaxed above the crown of your head with palms upward and the bottoms of your palms touching, to create a lotus formation. Draw the hands down the sides of your head slowly, then down to your chest to mix the energy with yours, finally releasing your hands to your sides in the dola mudra posture to represent dispersing any excess energies from your body harmlessly into the earth, leaving only what is sacred behind.

You can visualize the energy washing over you as if you were bursting a water balloon on your head.

Invoking the Divine Masculine and the Divine Feminine Together

This invocation can be done alone or with a partner. Sometimes spirit can feel so big that one cannot fit all of it into one category. That is why so many spiritual practices have the concept of polarity; the sacred is in two parts that unite as one. Consider the yin-yang symbol. The two different colored parts work together to form a cohesive whole. Honoring both the male and female aspects of the divine can be one way to bring balance and harmony to your spiritual practice if it resonates with you. Ideally, this can be done with a partner for one to represent the male aspect and one to represent the female, but the actual genders or sexualities of the participants do not matter for the purposes of this exercise.

With a partner, start out side by side with your closest arm around your partner and the other hand free to make the mudra. Both of you should raise your hands above your head in ardhachandra, a flat hand with the thumb out at a 90-degree angle. Now, connect your hands together at the thumbtips and the tips of your index fingers so that the two mudras together form a triangle. Breathe deeply together with your partner and part your hands at the same time, mirroring each other as you extend your arm out and around, taking your ardhachandra in a semicirclular arc beside your body and then crossing your hand in front of your body to unite with your partner again to form another triangle, this time with it pointing downward. You can also slowly chant the phrase "As above, so below," a famous magical phrase by Hermes Trismegistus that emphasizes that what happens in one reality happens in all others. Thoughts are things, and what you dream up you can manifest into reality. The dance of the universe above matches ours here on Earth, and the actions of the divine are our actions too, since the divine is always within.

Without a partner, you can perform this exercise with two hands by first forming the upward triangle mudra above your head. Breathe deeply and chant, "As above, so below," as you part your hands, extending them out to your sides and then connecting them together again around your navel to form a downward-pointing triangle. This works just as well as a spiritual exercise without a partner, but with a partner you can use this as a bonding activity. Note that you do not need to be in a romantic relationship with the partner for this exercise to work to create harmony between you.

Mudras and Candle Magic

In ancient times, people danced around a fire to raise energy and make magic happen in their lives. In modern movies and video games, witches cast fireballs and lightning with their hands as they interact with people and objects. However, in most modern candle magic spellbooks, the instructions say to light a colored candle and walk away with little more than a prayer. Certainly, that's enough to do the trick for many people and many situations. However, adding a mudra or two for flair can boost any candle magic.

There are three techniques for candle magic that can be aided by mudras: dressing the candle (that is, anointing it with oil), blessing the candle, and sending the magic of the candle out in the world to make manifest your desires. In some candle magic, sending the magic is not necessary, depending on the point of the magic. To teach candle magic with mudras, I will first show you a generic candle magic ritual, one that I do most frequently. Then, I will teach you the different mudras that can be used for each of the three candle magic techniques described above. After that, I will give several other specific examples of candle magic rituals for certain intentions so that you can see how different mudras may be chosen for your different intentions. That way, when you've seen what I've laid out in this book, you'll be able to design and create your own candle magic spells with mudras.

Universal Candle Magic Spell Booster

The real magic of candle magic begins after you've selected the color of candle that best suits your needs. A white candle, much like a white dress, goes well with anything. Next, you dress the candle with oil. Candle dressing is even more important than lighting the candle, for magical purposes. After all, people light candles every day with no thought about magical effect. Choose or make your own candle oil that suits your purpose. A good generic

oil is grapeseed oil with frankincense essential oil or with crushed frankincense steeped in it.

To apply the dressing oil to the candle, put a few drops of oil in your
palms. Form your hands into chatura mudra by tucking the candle under the
thumbs of each hand and lifting your pinkie finger. With this grasp, beginning at the middle of the candle, rub the oil onto the outside of the candle
by twisting your hands in opposite directions and pulling them toward the
opposite ends of the candle. With this gesture, you will have wiped some of
the oil from your palms onto the candle. While you do so, contemplate the
intention with which you would like to bless this candle.

Next, light the candle in a safe candle holder on an altar or some other
place of importance where you can supervise your candle's burn. With your
pointer finger (suchi mudra), draw the following fire invoking pentagram
safely high enough above the burning candle flame that you don't singe your
hands. Don't forget to trace the final line as a repeat of the first line, so that
that one line is "drawn" twice.

This gesture boosts the power of your candle magic by aiding the fire's energy
to manifest your desires. Immediately after drawing the pentagram, form
both hands into chandrakala mudra, which is simply a flat hand with thumb
sticking out perpendicular to the fingers. Gesture with the hands to pull the
energy from the pentagram that you've drawn slowly down over the candle,
at a safe distance, of course. Move your hands as if you're carefully lowering a
delicate glass bell jar over the candle and resting it there. You have now fully
blessed the candle with energy. Remember not to let it burn unattended. If
you would like to burn it multiple times, extinguish it with a candle snuffer

and repeat the pentagram and chandrakala blessing each time you light it. It is not necessary to repeat the candle dressing.

Candle Dressing Gestures

Now that you've seen what candle magic looks like with mudras, I'll break down the different options that you can use as building blocks for your own candle rituals. The specific ritual examples that I'll include after this breakdown will help you see what the final product can look like for highly customized candle magic. Let's start with the candle dressing gestures, all of which can be used to apply oil with either the palm or the fingertips.

Padmakosha and Kangula: Apply oil to your fingertips and form your hands into these mudras to impart divine feminine energy. This mudra helps with oil dressing for spells for childbirth, fertility, alleviating menstrual pain, emotional healing, divination, psychic power, solving mysteries, and receiving abundance.

Simhamukha: Apply oil to your fingertips and dress the candle with this mudra to impart divine masculine energy. This mudra helps with candle dressing for success, leadership, business dealings, resolving conflict, setting limits, and finding direction.

Chatura: Apply oil with your palms as in the earlier Universal Candle Magic Spell Booster to dress your candle for alleviating grief, financial windfalls, letting go, receiving gifts, and glamour spells making yourself appear to others as more beautiful or convincing.

Candle Blessing and Sending Gestures

Drawing a pentagram with the pointer finger (suchi mudra) is a flexible blessing that can be modified for different purposes with the direction that you draw the pentagram. Even if you choose another candle blessing mudra, these pentagrams can be carved into the candle's wax. There are five different ways that you can draw a pentagram to bless a candle, some with a couple of different meanings depending on the intention you hold in your head and in your heart.

Invoking and Banishing Pentagrams

Air Invoking/Water Banishing: Inspiration, emotional stability, meditation, and mindfulness.

Fire Invoking: Dynamic power, generativity, transformation, passion, and men's mysteries.

Fire Banishing: Tamping down destructive forces and ridding the self of obsessions.

Water Invoking/Air Banishing: Intuition, emotional atonement, and healing.

Earth Invoking: Abundance, stability, money magic, growing things, and women's mysteries.

Earth Banishing: Protection, hex breaking, exorcism, and ghost busting.

Chandrakala

As in the Universal Magic Candle Spell Booster, hands in this mudra can be drawn down the sides of the candle to bless it with the powerful energy of the moon reaching its fullness for abundance, success, prosperity, psychic power, and completion.

Ardhachandra

With the same movement as chandrakala, hands in ardhachandra can bless a candle with the energy of new beginnings, and magic that is meant to take hold and grow in someone's life for quite some time.

Sign of the Goddess

Bless the candle with hands in the sign of the Goddess to add the power of the divine feminine for mother energy, beauty, love, and intuition.

Kapotam

Kapotam can both bless the candle and send the spell. To do this, hold kapotam over the candle's flame, then split your hands apart to draw them down the sides of the candle to bless it. When your hands reach the surface on which the candle is resting, slide them forward, away from your body, as if shoving the candle's magic that you've now wrapped up neatly in an energetic package. This mudra directs the energy toward its most practical solution and is useful if you're not sure how the problem will be solved, or if you're sending the energy to a loved one by giving it a gentle push in his or her direction.

Bramara

Use this mudra to send the spell by moving the bramara mudra over the candle's flame, allowing your hands to rise while waggling at the wrists and then releasing the mudra high up in the air over your head. While you're doing this, visualize a swarm of bees carrying your spell to whomever needs it. This gesture is useful for spells cast upon an entire community for peace or healing.

Eagle Seal (Garuda Mudra)

Send the spell with the eagle seal if you are blessing a person or a place with a location you can't pinpoint on a map. As you form the eagle over the candle's flame, allow your hands to rise and release the mudra above your head, as with bramara. As you do, visualize the eagle seeking out the spell's target and landing there.

Prana and Stars

To send a spell with this gesture, form your dominant hand into the prana mudra by touching your thumb and forefinger together. Hold it above the candle's flame, and allow your hand to rise while you flick your thumb and finger three times in a gentle arc. The three flicks of the mudra represent stars formed in the sky. Use this mudra if you're using the candle to bless a room or a space that the candle occupies. The energetic stars will hang in the air long after the candle has burned down completely. The thoughtforms you have created act like a signpost directing the energies and attentions of positive entities.

Chakram

Seal and send a spell with chakram by holding your hands a safe distance above the flame. Palms are flat and pressed together with thumbs out. Begin the motion with your right-hand fingers skyward and your left-hand fingers pointing forward. Rotate your hands against each other to change position, representing the turning of a wheel, ending with your left hand's fingers skyward and your right hand's fingers forward. Use this gesture for spells that involve karma, cycles, endings, new beginnings, travel, and banishing.

Candle Magic Spell Example: Glamour Spell

You don't need makeup if you have magic to enhance your appearance. Glamour spells are popular among newcomers to magic because of the potential to see startling results in the mirror. More importantly, glamour spells become valuable and effective in situations where you want to be perceived in your best light. Use this glamour spell before a first date, a job interview, or an important speech.

Procure a small new candle, preferably gold in color to represent eye-catching confidence and optimism.

Steep dried rose petals in grapeseed oil to help make the metaphorical rose-colored glasses that help the glamour spell work. Apply oil with chatura mudra. As you dress the candle, visualize yourself as you want to be seen, and hear yourself speaking with a silver tongue. After lighting the candle, bless it with the sign of the Goddess for beauty. Let the candle burn out completely.

Candle Magic Spell Example: Peace Spell

A peace spell candle can be lit for a community in conflict or a politician with a troubled mind. Use a white candle dressed with grapeseed oil in which coriander or dried chamomile flowers have been steeped. Apply the oil with your fingertips while you form the simhamukha mudra, so you will be keeping your pinkies and index fingers out. Visualize the ideal outcome of your spell. What does this peaceful community or person look like and sound like if everything turns out right? Draw a fire banishing pentagram starting at the bottom right corner and finishing at the top when you've redrawn the first line. Bless the candle with this energy by forming your hands into ardhachandra by sticking out your thumb and forefinger and pulling them slowly down off to the sides of the candle at a safe distance. Finish sending this peace spell to your target(s) using bramara mudra at a safe distance above the candle. For each hand separately, curl your index fingers in while connecting the fingertips of your middle fingers and thumbs. Waggle your wrists and let this image of the bumblebee soar into the air and disperse as you raise your hands and release the mudra. You can snuff and relight this candle on subsequent days, repeating ardhachandra and bramara at each lighting. No need to dress the candle again between lightings. This exercise is ideal for before a daily peace meditation practice.

Candle Magic Spell Example: Emotional Strength for a Distant Friend

"I'll light a candle for you!" You write the message on social media to a loved one who is going through a complicated and difficult challenge. Here are some mudras that will superpower your candle magic and give your friend a boost if they choose to accept the energy. Begin with a small white tealight candle on which you can inscribe the initials of your friend in the wax. Use grapeseed oil steeped with lavender or lavender essential oil. Apply the oil to the tips of your fingers and dress the candle while forming your hands into the kangula mudra by curling your index fingers into your palm. Visualize your friend feeling at peak wellness. After lighting the candle, link your thumbs to form the eagle seal (garuda), moving your hands as if making a bird shadow puppet safely over the candle's flame, lifting up into the sky to release the mudra. Allow the candle to burn down completely, and the spell is cast.

Candle Magic Spell Example: Honoring the Dead

This spell can be adapted to honor a specific loved one on a special day of the year, such as their birthdate, their death date, or an anniversary, or during cultural festivities to honor the dead. In such a case, you can choose a small candle in the deceased's favorite color to burn on the special day. This spell is made, however, to bless one's ancestors in general and to ask for their blessings in return. For this reason, it is often best to set up a permanent or semipermanent shrine space on a table or shelf with photos of the deceased. Offerings such as water and bits of food can be provided, and a large black candle can be lit nightly. Dress the candle with frankincense oil using the chatura mudra by sticking out your pinkie fingers. As you dress the candle, chant any names of your mighty dead ancestors that you know, ending with, "and any unnamed, known or unknown." Each time you light the candle, seal it with the prana and stars gesture (see page 123) with your dominant hand. Form the prana mudra by touching your index finger to your thumb, and then flick your fingers in the air three times a safe distance over the candle's flame. You have now invited your ancestors to watch over you and your space.

Candle Magic Spell Example: Drawing Love

Love spells have been used for thousands of years, but they sit in an ethical gray area. One could argue the point that forcing a specific person to love you would not be true love at all. However, this candle magic spell is designed to work on you, rather than a specific crush. Instead, let's turn you into a beacon of attraction to draw the attention of your next great romance partner. It is best to light this candle on the full moon. Start with a small pink candle onto which you have inscribed your initials. Dress the candle with grapeseed oil in which rosemary has been steeped. Use the chatura mudra. As you do so, chant some of the words that you would like your next relationship to demonstrate, such as trust, love, kindness, equality, and so on. Light the candle and finish with the Goddess mudra blessing by curving your pointer finger and thumb into a letter *C* with each hand and drawing them slowly down either side of the candle at a safe distance as if creating a cylinder surrounding the candle. Allow the candle to burn down completely, if possible, to complete the spell. You can go about your regular life, but it is up to you to identify and act on the potential love opportunities that will now be drawn your way.

Candle Magic Spell Example: Money Luck

Money spells are also best performed on a full moon. This particular money spell is designed to draw increased streams of money over time, rather than one big financial windfall. Use a money luck candle spell during times when you need a little luck added to every little financial decision. The candle can be placed in a place of business or next to one's computer as one invests online. Prepare an oil of cinnamon, galangal, or orange rinds. Apply oil to a large green candle with your fingertips while holding simhamukha mudra by raising your index and pinkie fingers. Visualize your life in the comfort of financial security. It is important not to ruminate on the process of making money, because that limits the universe's avenues through which blessings can arrive. Instead, picture yourself as already wealthy, whatever wealth looks like to you. After lighting the candle, draw an earth invoking pentagram safely above the flame and use hands flat in chandrakala with thumbs out to push down to either side of the candle to bless it. When you can't supervise the candle, safely snuff it instead of burning it out. Repeat the pentagram and chandrakala blessing briefly each time you light it.

Candle Magic Spell Example: Light of Justice

Sometimes it may feel like karma needs a boost; that is, some situation in your life or the life of someone you care about requires swift justice. Light this candle before an important trial, hearing, arbitration, or even an evaluation to see fairness applied quickly. All the truth will become clear with this spell, so do not perform it unless you want the bad facts to come out with the good. This is not a glamour spell, so it won't make you look better in front of a judge if you're in the wrong. The right decision for all concerned will be boosted and made more probable.

Procure a black candle. Apply oil in which crushed bay leaf has been steeped, with the fingers of your hands shaped in simhamukha mudra. As you dress the candle, meditate on the image of balanced scales of justice or an endless knot. Clear every other thought from your mind except this image. When it is time to light the candle, form the kapotam mudra at a safe height over the candle's flame, and then bring your hands down to either side of the candle until they meet the table, sliding your hands forward to send the spell. Burn the candle during each moment when you want your case to be at the forefront of the minds of those adjudicating the matter. Snuff the candle rather than blowing it out between lightings. Each time you light it, repeat the kapotam sending gesture. There is no need to redress the candle every time.

Spells for Everyday Life

Your hands are your tools for magic anywhere you go. Through mudras, you can make magic without the candles, crystals, smells, and bells that require the expense and time of obtaining supplies. Of course, added supplies can help boost your intentions and improve the spells. But your hands remain the Swiss Army knife of moving spiritual energy. The lack of additional necessities for magic makes mudra spells ideal for places like hospitals or dormitories where open flame, incense, or other supplies are forbidden. Paring down the extravagance of spells and ritual encourages you to add a spiritual flair to your everyday life by keeping magic simple and accessible. Learning the mudras ensures that, even if you are ever in an environment that is incompatible with or even hostile to certain magical tools, you will have an alternative that nobody will ever take away from you.

Imbibing Spell for Peace, Healing, or Confidence

Much like candle magic, this spell format requires simple extra materials and can be used for a variety of intentions. During this spell, you are going to infuse water with your intentions and then drink it. The symbolic act of drinking in your intentions and allowing them to be put to use within your body makes this spell ideal for the purposes of peace, healing, or self-confidence. It is vital to choose a single intention before beginning this spell. Too many intentions will muddle the results. Though best performed at the full moon, this spell can work at any time and is suitable for using when taking daily medications for healing.

Begin with a small glass of water and freshly washed hands. Extend two fingers of your dominant hand to form the padmakosha mudra and stir the water clockwise with your dominant hand. As you stir the water, visualize what you would look like, sound like, and act like if you had achieved your intention. For example, if you want to have inner peace, see yourself in your mind's eye speaking peaceful words or meditating in nature. For healing, see an image of yourself at full health. For inner confidence, picture how you would walk with confidence, what deeds you would do, and what strong words you would share. When you have completed stirring the water at least three times, remove your hand from the water. Form both of your hands into arala mudra with palms flat, thumbs in line with the palm, and index fingers bent forward at the second joint. Keeping your hands in that position, as much as is practical, use both hands to pick up the glass and drink the water. The spell is done.

Signs to Make to Ward Off Sickness
or to Cause Illness to Leave the Body

Of course, no mudra can be relied upon to cure any disease without the intervention of qualified medical professionals, and yet mudras have been used to help heal and protect against disease. Washing your hands is the best thing that you can do to prevent infectious disease, so be sure to do that before practicing these mudras. If you want to make a subtle sign when you find yourself in an infectious environment, like public transit during flu season or a room full of preschoolers, use the surya mudra. Hold your ring finger to your palm with your thumb. To make a mudra even more discreet, hide it in a pocket with your nondominant hand.

Surya can be used to elevate your body temperature, which stimulates your immune system. For most effective use, you should "inoculate" yourself by meditating and practicing your intention to raise your body temperature. I remember, as a child, I could make myself have a fever to get to go home from school early. At the time, I would make myself cry, since that did the trick. Theoretically, if I had held surya mudra every time that I successfully raised my body temperature, I would condition my brain and body to make the connection, and recall it more easily with surya in the future. Even if you're not a naughty schoolchild, it can be beneficial to practice with surya to strengthen your body-mind connection before using it out in the wild.

Perform this inoculation meditation for fifteen minutes daily, if possible. Sit or lie down if you will be using the accompanying breath control. This is a good one to add to your daily meditation rotation during cold and flu season. Hold surya with your nondominant hand. This is good practice since, many times, when using surya out in the world, you might be shaking hands with someone or holding a pen or something with your dominant hand. During the meditation, you'll use your dominant hand to hold the lung (or bronchial) mudra that is made by pressing the tips of your index, middle, and ring fingers into three points on your thumb so that you can feel the pressure.

Accompany your mudras with breath control meant to aid elevated temperature in extreme conditions. While you meditate to raise body temperature, if your body feels comfortable with breathing exercises, practice taking deep breaths for about two minutes and allowing them to flow out of you quickly without forcing them, as if slowly panting. Then, exhale to hold "empty" lungs as long as you can practically do so. Then, take a deep breath and hold full lungs for as long as you can practically do so. Repeat the entire breathing exercise, starting over from the panting breaths again, as many times as feels comfortable, knowing that practice will expand your capabilities. Make sure not to hyperventilate during this process by listening to your body, and remain seated or lying down in case you feel light-headed.

Mudra Exercise for Remembering Your Dreams

Do you struggle to remember your dreams when you awaken? If you struggle to remember your dreams when you awaken, you might even be one of those people who wonders if they dream at all. Everyone with healthy sleep patterns does dream, but sometimes the memories of them disappear so quickly when we wake up that it's impossible to remember them. This exercise is best performed after the Healthy Sleep Meditation found on page 94. As soon as you awaken, simply make the khattva mudra with both hands by extending your pinkie and pointer fingers to form the legs of a bed, touching the middle and ring fingers of one hand to the other hand's corresponding fingers to form the mattress, and folding your thumbs in to form the headboard and footboard. As soon as you make this gesture, sit up in bed and either verbally state what you remember from your dreams or, preferably, break the mudra to write down everything you remember. It's okay if you only remember brief snippets, such as a color, a place, a person, an animal, or an object. Over time and with practice and diligence, your recall will improve.

Spell to Come to Agreement

A simple, meditative spell may be what is needed to help settle a dispute. The best people to perform this spell upon are yourself and someone you love whom you want to keep in your life. Since working spiritually with someone may tie yourself energetically to him or her, it's best not to do this spell to settle an argument with an annoying coworker or a neighbor who you just wish would move away. Magic works best when you change your own perception of the world at large, rather than trying to make puppets of others. You can't force your dad to give you the car with this spell, but you can certainly cast an energy of peace over your negotiations that may incline his mind to agree and will certainly make it easier for you to accept a compromise. The only supplies you need for this spell are a washable pink marker and your own two hands.

Please note that a spell to come to agreement is not the best thing to try to employ in the heat of a fresh argument. For that sort of work, I'd advise the Angry Argument Meditation found on page 90. The Spell to Come to Agreement is better for a planned deliberation, such as a mediation appointment, an intervention, or plans to change someone's living situation. It is okay if you feel some anxiety about the impending debate or ultimatum, but the spell doesn't work well when performed on impulse since it works directly to counteract brash impulsiveness.

Prepare yourself for meditation and write your name on the palm of your dominant hand and your opponent's name on your nondominant hand. Begin the meditation by forming your hands into bherunda, and then crossing them at the wrist. To do this mudra, curl your index fingers over the tops of the thumbs and allow the rest of the fingers to press into your palm. As you sit or lie down with wrists crossed, mentally scan your body for any sensations of tightness. Relax your shoulders. Relax your jaw. Relax your forehead. Allow your tongue to drop from the roof of your mouth. When you have consciously turned yourself to all those tense parts of your body, slowly uncross your wrists, keeping the mudra in each hand. Settle your hands on your knees and try to hold your inner peace and a blank mind for the remainder of your meditation period. Ideally, the entire meditation should last twenty minutes, from start to finish.

Charm to Strengthen Justice in Court

Here is a mudra that can be used as a simple charm to encourage justice in a courtroom and increase your personal confidence. You will be taking a deep breath and exhaling gently down into your hands to "blow" your inner truth outward to the judge. Start by forming the inner vision mudra, to help amplify the most pragmatic truth that you carry within yourself. Interlace the knuckles of your pointer and middle fingers, right over left, and touch your thumbs together. The mudra can rest inconspicuously in front of you, appearing to merely be folded hands. During the hearing or trial, you can breathe deeply, and surreptitiously breathe slowly and softly out and down-ward toward your hands. When you feel you have done your best and wish to complete the charm, move your hands briefly in chakram by rotating your palms against one another, right hand clockwise and left hand counterclock-wise, before dropping the mudra.

Gambling Good Luck Charm

We've seen in the movies when gamblers blow on dice before rolling them, or cross the fingers of both hands. An alternative good luck gesture that is more discreet is called "pressing thumbs." With both hands, make a fist and tuck your thumbs inside your fists. There is another gesture, the mano fico, that can be done for good luck, but it can also be problematic due to lewd conno-tations. The mano fico and other strong protection against misfortune will be discussed further in the next chapter.

Good Luck Ritual

Many of us have heard the phrase "knock on wood," often accompanied with the gesture of rapping a fist on the closest presumed wooden surface. The purpose of the protective knocking gesture is to ward off any chance of being smote by divine wrath for the hubris of saying something ironic or presump-tive. It is time to learn about the real good luck ritual of knocking on wood, which has little to do with knocking on a chair or table and much to do with the forest spirits who live in trees. Knocking on wood is done twice: the first knock is to make a wish, appealing to the nature spirits, and the second is to thank the spirits for granting your wish. When doing magic, it is okay to knock in quick succession without checking to see that your wish has been granted, because assuming that you have already manifested the world you want is part of performing effective magic.

A simple, common spell is done with a willow tree. Go to a weeping wil-low tree. Form your hand into the mano fico, or fig gesture, by making a fist and sticking your thumb out between the index and middle fingers. Knock once on the bark of the trunk. Then, tie a brightly colored ribbon to one of the branches and gently tie a knot with the flexible tip of the weeping willow branch while speaking your wish. Knock once more on the trunk and say your thanks. When you verify that your wish has been well and truly granted, return to the tree to untie the knot and remove the ribbon. The point of the ribbon is to act as a tourniquet to keep the forest spirits from the knotting area so that they aren't harmed by the knot, and the bright colors help you locate the branch you used when you return. Trust me, it is hard to pick out a tiny knot in a multitude of leafy weeping willow branches, especially if some time or seasons have passed between your visits to the tree.

~4~
Mudras in Ritual

Now that you've learned about some ritual building blocks, I'll give you a full ritual that you can use either to forge a deeper connection with spirit or to manifest your desires by inserting any particular mudra meditation or mudra charging you would like to use. You can also insert spells, which you'll find on page 127 in the section headed "Spells for Everyday Life." Since most people reading this book are beginners with different strengths and needs, I've filled this general ritual with many parts that can be changed or omitted by the beginner if it feels too complicated. I have purposely left out any physical tools or offerings (though you can add any bells and whistles that you like) because tools should not be a crutch. You'll also notice the absence of any words, as they too are merely tools. This leaves you space to use your own meaningful words or to explore using just your body and your mind to create ritual. I'll explain each component so that you can decide for yourself how you'd like your ritual life to look. This is a general catchall, workhorse ritual that can be used for everything from a wedding to a daily devotional. Ritual duration can last between thirty minutes and several hours depending on what sacred activities you add.

Greater Universal Rite of Worship and Magic

Step 1: Begin at the Beginning—Call the Rite to Order

Form the shankha mudra to begin the rite, as if you were blowing a conch shell to summon the attention of all the good spirits that you would want to join you in this place at this time. Grip the thumb of your left hand with your right and fold your right hand around your left hand to form the seashell shape. Take a deep, centering breath through your nose and blow it out slowly through your mouth.

Step 2: Sweep Out Any Negative Energy from Your New Sacred Space

Walk counterclockwise in a circle three times around the space, using padmakosha to sweep the air. This mudra cups your fingers to form a bell-like shape. Bells and brooms have symbolically been used to cleanse physical space of negative energies, which is an important beginning to any ritual in which you want to create and send positive magic into the world. You can begin and end the circle in the east to symbolize new beginnings, as that is where the sun rises at dawn.

Step 3: Cast the Circle

Drawing an imaginary circle defines your newly cleaned sacred space so that no negative energy can rush in and you can manifest whatever you desire. Using a pointed finger (suchi mudra), walk around your space clockwise, drawing a circle in your mind's eye. Again, you can begin and end in the east to symbolize new beginnings. Traditionally, incense and holy water are often walked around the circle to disperse at this stage, but in this example our mudras are our offerings.

Step 4: Call the Quarters

Now that you have a blank space that you have set up for spiritual activity, this circle becomes your sandbox for creating your dreams. But first, we must invite the ingredients we need and set up our own little world. Calling the quarters is the act of gathering the ingredients, which are the four mystical elements of earth, air, fire, and water. Ancient peoples believed that the four elements were the building blocks for everything in the universe, and we still use them symbolically today. Calling the quarters also sets up your own little world, your little microcosm, that has its own north, south, east, and west on the map. Here is how to gather the ingredients to craft your world.

Air: Face east. Hold hands at chest height with your palms facing away from you. This is a simple gesture indicating the gentle push of air. Air represents inspiration and new beginnings. Imagine a gentle wind of change pushing back upon your hands. Perform the sign for unity, balance, completion (see page 116). As a quick reminder, this sign is made by bringing your hands back in as if you are gathering that air energy to your chest and then thrusting them back outward with palms out and fingertips up. Repeat this gathering and thrusting motion with your arms three times toward the east.

Fire: Face south. Lift your hands above your head with elbows straight and hands balled into fists. This gesture emphasizes the transformative power of fire. Imagine fiery strength contained within your fists. Then, spread your fingers again to perform the sign for unity, balance, completion. The sign is done identically to the previous step, even though this time you will be gathering fire energy, again ending with palms out and fingertips up. You will end the three repetitions of this motion still facing south.

Water: Face west. Hold your hands at the height of your face, cupping them as if to contain water. Imagine that your hands are filled with the cooling, healing water that sustains all life. Perform the sign for unity, balance, completion in the same manner that you did toward the other two directions.

Earth: Face north. Hold your hands at the height of your waist with your palms downward in pataka. Imagine that your hands mark the horizon and that you are pressing down upon the firm, solid Mother Earth. Perform the sign for unity, balance, completion.

Step 5: Pray to the Divine

You've done it! Now that you have created a sacred space between the worlds and filled it with all the potential of the universe, it is time to invite the divine to pay a special visit to you to bless your space and yourself. This part of the ritual is very flexible since your own understanding of spirit may be much different from mine. If you have devotional words, hand positions, or movements that you feel called to do here to invite your divine spirit or higher self, please opt for any that already work for you. That said, here are a few examples that you can use or adapt to your own faith tradition. I have included references to the divine feminine, the divine masculine, and the unknowable force of spirit. Feel free to use all of them or none of them as suits you. The default direction to face during this part of the ritual is toward the east to welcome in energies.

Spiritual Freedom: The spiritual freedom hand pose is a general mudra that helps plug you into the aspect of spirit that is omnipotent, boundless, and often abstract. This gesture is well suited for calling upon your higher self or for acknowledging the unknowable mysteries of the divine before calling upon individual deities with whom you may have a relationship. The spiritual freedom mudra is also suitable for agnostics or seekers still exploring their faith with more questions than answers. To make the spiritual freedom mudra, use both hands with palms facing away from you, held flat with the ring finger folded over perpendicular to your palm. Remember to keep your thumbs pressed in alignment with your fingers. To give this sign a little motion, you can waggle your hands slightly at your wrists to make it appear like you are holding two dancing flames. Hold this mudra as high as is comfortable for your body.

Sign of the Goddess: To invoke the divine feminine, raise your left hand as high as is comfortable. Use your index finger and thumb to shape a letter C and tuck your remaining fingers away into your palm. Gaze up at this crescent moon that you've formed in the sky and visualize the form of the divine feminine that calls to you.

Sign of the Horns: To invoke the divine masculine, raise your right hand as high as you can and make the sign of the horns by extending your index and pinkie fingers to the sky and trapping the remaining fingers onto your palm with your thumb. As you look at this mudra, call to mind your own personal vision of God.

Step 6: This Is Where You Insert Any Meditation, Mudra Charging, or Spell If You Wish

You have made it to the juicy, inner part of the ritual. If the beginning of this ritual is the first slice of bread while making a ritual sandwich, you are currently working on the meat of the sandwich. Depending on your ritual, you can put anything here that you like. If you are celebrating a wedding, this is where you would put the vows. If you would like to meditate or do trance work, you can use any of the exercises from chapter 2 at this point in the ritual. More exercises are included throughout this chapter as well.

Step 7: Receive Blessings from the Divine

Having done whatever magical work is necessary in your life right now, you can receive your blessings from the divine that you have invited to your ritual. Traditionally, this stage of ritual might involve food or beverages for both participants and as offering to spirit. However, for this ritual, the mudras become both our offerings and the connection to the divine through which we accept boons. Again, depending on your faith tradition, you may already have some spiritual or cultural practices that can fill in the blanks here better than my suggestions. Go ahead and run with your ideas. I've provided these here only because they do work, not because they're the only benedictions that work. I've provided a mudra and a moving gesture here, one to directly channel blessings if you happen to have a visible full moon in the sky, and one to receive and integrate blessings with your own soul any time. They can be used together or separately. After all, there is not always a full moon view on hand for the moon altar mudra. Take your time with this sacred and meaningful portion of the ritual. The most important thing is not what your hands are doing but that your heart and soul are open to sacred experience.

Moon Altar: For this mudra exercise to work best, you should have direct line of sight with a full moon. Otherwise, please skip to the sign for drawing blessings that follows. A more complete version of Drawing Power from the Moon is available in chapter 2, but here's an abbreviated reminder of the important points. The idea behind this practice is to channel divine blessings directly from this symbol of power, magic, mystery, and cycles of the universe. The full moon happens at a precise time that can be found for your locality, but the three days before and after the full moon also have enough full moon energy for this mudra. Ideally, you'd be performing this ritual outdoors, but this mudra also works just fine viewing the moon through a window. Begin by holding your hands next to one another with palms flat toward one another without touching them. Fold in your thumbs toward the insides of your palms and press them together at the two joints. Bend your thumb tips away from you at the joint to form a flat altar. Hold your hands so that the moon appears to rest on the altar formed by the thumbs. Find a comfortable position to gaze at the moon on your moon altar in brief meditation. Know that there is a mental link between you and the sacred aspects of the moon and allow yourself to draw energy through that connection into your body through your hands. You may sense a buildup of energy as a feeling of pressure, buzzing, an inner sense, or a vision in the mind's eye. When you sense that your experience of this energy has peaked or is sufficient, end the mudra by blowing two kisses to the moon with your dominant hand. Follow this mudra with the sign for drawing blessings or by at least grounding yourself with the dola mudra with your hands relaxed down and out to your sides.

Sign for Drawing Blessings: Immediately after or instead of the moon altar, you can bless yourself and fully merge divine energy with your own with this slow and graceful gesture. Hold your hands relaxed above the crown of your head with palms upward, the bottoms of your palms touching, and your fingertips spread to the sky. Your hands look like a crown or a lotus and are positioned at the top of your head, through which divine energy channels are believed to flow down into the rest of your body. In one slow, smooth motion move the hands down the sides of your head slowly, then down to your chest to mix the energy with yours, finally releasing your hands to your sides in the dola mudra posture. As your hands move down your body, visualize the energy pouring over and through you like water, suffusing every cell of your being with spirit. At the end of the gesture as your hands flop relaxed to your sides a little way out from your body, visualize any excess, stuck, or negative energies from your body dripping off your fingertips harmlessly into the earth. You should feel calm yet alert. If you feel drained or jittery, you can troubleshoot these energy perceptions by grounding before receiving blessings from the divine and spending more time grounding afterward.

Step 8: Close the Circle

You've set up an invisible but very powerful temple with your own two hands, but like packing up after camping, you must carefully close your ritual by thanking all the entities that have aided you and dismantling the potent energetic structure you may have just set up in your living room. You want to leave the space energetically just the way you found it, to avoid any unintended magical effects. You can always conjure it all back up again whenever you need it. Thankfully, closing the circle is quicker than setting it up, but you still need to work backward through some of the previous steps. In my faith tradition, we don't dismiss deities, but if your faith tradition involves thanking them and asking them to depart to their realms, do that first. Next, you will bid adieu to each of the four quarters by slowly extending the salute that you did to welcome them as you visualize seeing that energy on its way. As a reminder:

Air: Face east. Push hands out at chest height with your palms facing away from you.

Fire: Face south. Lift your fists above your head with elbows straight.

Water: Face west. Extend your cupped hands away from you at the height of your face.

Earth: Face north. Push your hands down, palms downward, at the height of
your waist.

Now that you have waved goodbye to the four directions, walk counterclockwise, beginning and ending in the west. If you happened to use things
like incense and holy water during the beginning of your ritual, now is the
time to use them again. Then, holding your dominant hand as a pointed finger (suchi mudra), extend your hand overhead and make a sweeping, cutting motion down through the wall of your circle boundary, visualizing the
energy collapsing like a tent or a bubble. Your rite is ended, and whatever
magic you've made has now been set in motion to manifest.

The Lesser Banishing Ritual of the Pentagram

Drawing pentagrams in the air has long been a powerful gesture in Western
magical tradition to both invoke and banish energies and, indeed, is often
used in rituals like the previous one to invite and dismiss the four elemental
quarters of earth, air, fire, and water. The purpose of the Lesser Banishing
Ritual of the Pentagram is to ward and send away any negative energy from
a space. Using a banishing ritual can be extremely useful in many contexts,
including resolving hauntings, blessing new homes, warding off nightmares,
or even making hotel rooms feel a little less foreign.

Ritual words feature prominently in the original version of the Lesser
Banishing Ritual of the Pentagram, but I have omitted them here too, as in
the previous ritual, for similar reasons. Remember, words are just a tool, but
it is the power of your magic and mind that is running this magic. This book
is all about focusing on mudras as your tool. Second, the original words are
steeped heavily in Judeo-Christian occultism, which may feel exclusionary
and uncomfortable for those of other spiritualities. Use words of your choice
or focus on making magic with your mudras.

One reason that the Lesser Banishing Ritual of the Pentagram works so
well is because every time an effective ritual is repeated, it makes a mark on
the collective unconscious, making each repetition easier and more effective, like a wagon wheel driving a shallow rut into the mud of a well-travelled

road. People have been reinforcing the Lesser Banishing Ritual of the Pentagram since the rise of the Golden Dawn in the late nineteenth century. For this reason, I've kept all the original ritual gestures and merely added embellishments to enhance them. Here's the LBRP in six simple steps:

Step 1: Prepare Yourself with the Body Integration Mudra

Stand facing east at the center of the room or space that you wish to cleanse. Form the body integration mudra by pressing your fists together at the knuckles at the height of your chest, allowing the tips or pads of your thumbs to connect above your fists. Visualize yourself as an expansive, enormous form in the cosmos. The earth beneath you is dwarfed by your presence. Above you, visualize the limitless power of the universe in your mind's eye. You might visualize it as a light, a color, a fluid, or any other imagery that works for you.

Step 2: Cross Your Body

Reach your dominant hand as high above your head as you can with your index and middle fingers pointed as high as they can go (ardhapataka mudra). This mudra represents a ritual dagger. Visualize slowly drawing that universal energy downward toward you as your hand moves downward. When you reach your head level, touch your thumb to those extended pointer and middle fingers, keeping your ring finger and pinkie curled into your palm. This is not a specific mudra, but is the most common hand position used by people when crossing themselves, and as you recall, the repetition of tradition can boost the effectiveness of this exercise. You will touch your body at your forehead and chest, ending with your hand at groin height with fingers pointing down as if the universal energy you have drawn is a column through your entire body. Next, as you touch first your right shoulder and then your left shoulder, visualize that energy radiating out each shoulder into space, so that there is a cross of this visualized energy that connects at the center of your chest. Spread your arms outward, then bring them up to connect them like prayer hands (anjali, namaskara, or salutation seal) above your head, and lower them so that you end this movement with hands pressed together in front of your chest.

Step 3: Pentagram

Turn and face east or walk to the eastern edge of the room or space. You're now going to draw a pentagram with a precisely defined visualization. Normally, I shy away from telling you exactly how and what to visualize, but in this case, there is value in following the tradition of those who have successfully worked this ritual so many times in the past. Extend your pointer finger (suchi mudra) and visualize drawing a flaming blue five-pointed star. Start your finger at the lower left-hand point, draw the entire five-pointed star, and finish the star by retracing that last line so that you end with your finger at the top point. See the flaming blue star clearly in your mind's eye before moving to the next step.

Step 4: Sign of the Enterer

Begin this movement with your hands to the sides of your heads with flat palms and thumbs up (chandrakala mudra). Take a deep breath and then, in one smooth motion as you exhale, step forward with your left foot and thrust your hands as if stabbing them right through the center of the flaming blue pentagram you have just drawn.

Step 5: Sign of Silence

Step back with your left foot to bring your feet back together. Withdraw your left hand to bring one finger to your lips (suchi, the sign of silence). Your right hand remains extended as you rotate ninety degrees to the right or walk to the southern edge of the room or space. Visualize drawing a line of energy as your extended right hand moves with you.

Repeat steps 3 through 5 for the south, west, and north.

Step 6: Hexagram

Return to the center of the room or space, facing east, and extend your arms, once again merging your body into the visualized cross of universal energy that you constructed at the beginning of the ritual. Clearly in your mind, visualize the entire energetic structure that you have constructed. There is a cross of visual energy within you that extends infinitely into all that exists, has existed, and is yet to exist. You have a solid circle of protection around you, warded in the four cardinal directions with shielding pentagrams. Add the final visualization, a beautiful six-sided hexagram star shining within you, and form the true self mudra atman in front of your chest right where the cross connects. Tent your fingers and then touch the first knuckles of your middle fingers together, allowing the thumbs to touch downward. You should have six fingertips skyward when forming the atman mudra.

Repeat step 2 to finish the ritual.

That's all there is to this ritual that has real staying power. You leave up the energetic structure you have constructed, so it keeps working. I tell my students that it is a little like those foaming cleaning agents with bubbles that "scrub" after you have applied them. Just a little work from you on this little standby ritual will keep up the protection energy for you in a space for quite some time. Ground yourself after this ritual if you find the sensation of the energy to feel too intense.

Storytelling for a Congregation, Coven, or Family

Myths and legends are an important part of spirituality for many people. While we know that many myths are not objectively true and were created by ancient peoples to explain their world, many myths have nuggets of spiritual truth that cannot be expressed well except as a story. Buddhists and Hindus are well known for including stories in their spiritual discourses. Christian leaders often share Bible stories to impart lessons and religious values. Story-telling has been a part of the human condition since before the written word.

Thus far, this book mostly has had exercises that can be done alone, though some can be performed with a partner. Using mudras for storytelling is best done with an audience, but it doesn't necessarily have to be a large audience. I have done spiritual storytelling for just my two children on occa-sion. Giving the audience a role or something to say or do can help people connect with any deep messages you want to share through your gestures. I will give a couple of examples of short spiritual stories, but first let me share with you a few simple components of ritual to make your own expression of divine myths something moving and memorable. Ideally, dramatic storytelling with mudras can become a useful creative outlet for you to build traditions with your loved ones or community of kindred spirits.

Spiritual Poetic Drama Building Blocks

Every story needs characters, and your mudras can transform you into multiple characters in a story with no costumes necessary. The gods in ancient Greek pottery can often be identified by the symbolic objects they're holding. For example, Zeus may hold a lightning bolt, making him unquestionably identifiable as the king of the gods who hurls lightning. The mudra equivalent of this concept can be seen with Hindu mythology. When a devotee wishes to perform as Ganesh, he or she may hold the kapitta mudra to represent his rattle with the hands at an angle away from the body to represent his large belly. When representing Shiva, one hand is held flat in blessing, while the other relaxes across the body in dola mudra and a leg is raised in a dancing pose. The goddesses Lakshmi and Parvati stand tall and hold the second version of katakaamukha to represent a lotus, while the goddess Durga might hold up three fingers to represent her trident. A simpler representation of the divine from Wiccan culture is to embody the God by standing tall with feet together, arms crossed at the chest with both hands in fists (mushthi mudra) to represent holding divine items, like Osiris holds his crook and flail. The Goddess pose is done with feet apart and hands spread out and to the sides with palms out and flat in blessing (pataka mudra). To switch characters during a story, use the simple technique of simply spinning around once and standing next to the place you stood a moment before. The gender of the character does not matter and performing cross-gender roles is just fine.

Example: Inviting Springtime Mudra Story for Family
This story is best performed about midway between the winter solstice and the spring equinox, around or about the first of February. This story requires

one character leading the ritual and portraying a goddess of spring and a participatory audience. The setting should ideally be at a family home.

The goddess circles the home three times and then knocks on the door three times. A member of the family audience opens the door for the goddess. She stands with feet apart. In her right hand she holds up one finger (suchi mudra) to represent a magic wand that she can wave to make springtime begin. In her left hand, she holds a representation of Brigid's Cross, using the second form of katakaamukha.

ALL: Welcome, springtime! Come in, come in, come in!

GODDESS: [Entering the home] In gratitude, I will bless you by making my bed here.

The goddess changes her hands to the khattvu mudra to represent her intention to rest in the home and bring springtime to the land. At this point, the goddess hugs each member of the family, then spins in a circle to become you, the member of your family once more.

ALL: [Raising hands high] The goddess is everywhere. [Spreading hands wide to your sides] The goddess is here in our home. [Bringing hands to chest] The goddess is here in our hearts.

Example: Winter Mudra Story for Spiritual Groups— The Holly King and the Oak King

A light-hearted and cheerful story, "The Holly King and the Oak King" should ideally be performed during the winter holidays for a larger gathering. Storytelling of this drama requires two characters who will engage in battle, representing the Holly King and the Oak King. This play works best if there is a stage or central performance area so that all can see.

The Holly King limps onto the stage, stooped over as if he is an elderly man. His hands are held atop his head with fingers spread to the sky (padmakosha mudra) to represent a crown. He moves as if to remove the crown from his head and his hands turn to tripataka mudra. Flat palms out with the ring finger bent

over perpendicular to the palm represent his claim over the land, and he blesses
the audience with spiritual freedom.

HOLLY KING: I am the Holly King, and I grow weary of my crown.

*The Oak King enters the scene. He strides tall and strong, confidently carrying
the nourisher (pushan) mudra. The right hand extends the index and pinkie
fingers. The left hand extends the ring and the pinkie fingers.*

OAK KING: I am the Oak King, and I will challenge you for your crown.

*The Holly King and the Oak King wage an epic battle. Have fun with this
scene! Using props like foam or cardboard swords is encouraged. In the end, the
wounded Holly King stages a dramatic death. The Oak King symbolically picks
up the Holly King's crown by taking on the padmakosha mudra and placing it on
his head. He can then take a bow and be cheered by the audience for ushering in
the upcoming change of seasons.*

Soul Retrieval Exercise

The trance work known as "soul retrieval" is a remedy for spiritual affliction, most commonly to fix a feeling of being too emotionally tied to another
human being. Trance work is a form of meditation that you may have already
tried during the automatic writing exercise on page 154 under the subheading "Receiving Psychic Messages from the Divine or the Departed." When
you are in a trance, you are able to reach the innermost part of your psy-
che: the right half of your brain that speaks in symbols and the subconscious
part of you that comes alive when you dream. In a sense, you're practicing
self-hypnosis. I decided not to include soul retrieval in the meditations chapter because it is not a ritual to be performed every day. If you're not sure that
you require soul retrieval, it's not necessary to try it. Even I was not truly
convinced about the process of soul retrieval until I needed it myself. Now, I
include a simplified version here so that everyone can benefit from it.

The theory behind soul retrieval is that, in your past, you gave a small
piece of yourself away. Typically, you left that soul shard with someone when
you made an agreement with him or her. This agreement might be a sacred

vow or promise, or it might merely have been an implicit agreement with no words involved. Whether it was made voluntarily and enthusiastically, or under duress from yourself or others, the agreement no longer serves you and your highest purpose. During the process of soul retrieval, you will enter a trance state and then mentally go back to the moments in time when you first made the agreement. In your mind's eye, you will take back a symbol of that agreement that represents the soul shard you gave away. Upon reintegrating that symbol with yourself through visualization and mudras, you will heal yourself of spiritual affliction and limitations, thus making your soul whole through soul retrieval. There are other, more drastic forms of soul retrieval that may be necessary for other situations, but this one helped me, and it can help you too.

Step 1: Cut Ties with Kartarimukha Mudra

The first step when trying to remediate a toxic connection with another person is to metaphorically cut ties with him or her. Don't worry if the person is somebody you love. Cutting the umbilical cord, so to speak, will not make it impossible for you to love each other in the future. Cutting energetic ties merely protects your own spiritual autonomy. The exercise here is a visualization one, but depending on the nature of your problem, you may find it prudent to cut communications and other contact with the person if necessary. To visualize cutting ties, hold your hands as if they are scissors (kartarimukha mudra). See, in your mind's eye, the cord of energy that ties you to the problematic person. Cut through this cord with your hand and see its destruction. Usually, this step is enough, but if the energetic cord appears to grow back, either immediately or over time, a full soul retrieval may be required. A more complete exercise for cutting ties is included in chapter 6, but this is a summary of a brief cutting of ties that can be repeated if you have done the full exercise before and noticed the ties return.

Step 2: Soul Retrieval with Bliss Mudra

Form the heart-shaped bliss mudra by touching the knuckles of your index fingers together and touching the knuckles of your middle and ring fingers to their counterparts as well. Your thumbs touch below to form the point of the heart. As you meditate holding the bliss mudra, think about your past with the person from whom you are trying to retrieve your soul shard. Take your time to consider all the agreements that you've made with that person, implicitly or explicitly, and how those limitations are affecting you today. You may arrive at one or more moments in time when you started performing some maladaptive behavior to protect yourself. Address each of those agreements separately. When you have homed in on the moment from your past, put yourself fully into the memory by rebuilding the moment from its surroundings. Where were you when it was happening? What were the sights, sounds, and smells of the moment? How old were you and what time of year was it? Replay the moment in your mind and allow yourself to see, in your mind's eye, a symbolic gift from your higher self that you can take back from this moment as you consciously revoke the agreement. It might be a jewel or other precious object, something intangible like a colored glowing light, or anything else. Reach out with your dominant hand with the prana mudra (hamsasya) as if to pick up the object with your thumb and forefinger. No matter how large, heavy, or awkward the object would be to manipulate in real life, in your mind's eye you can easily pinch it into near nothingness in your hand.

Step 3: Breathe and Connect with Your Soul

The full follow-up meditation is described on page 88 under the subheading "Breathe and Connect with Your Soul." With your soul shard pinched firmly in your dominant hand and your nondominant hand on your heart, begin slowly breathing with the following mudra movement. Hold the hand in front of your chest with your pinched fingers up and the back of your hand facing down. Draw your hand down as if you were unzipping a zipper. When you reach your navel, rotate the back of your hand upward to reverse the motion as if you were zipping up a zipper. When you reach the crown of your head, repeat the downward movement. Breathe in and out with the movement until you feel like the soul retrieval has successfully integrated with your energetic being. If you still feel oppressed by the other person's energy, you may need to revisit additional agreements or to take further practical steps to cut yourself off from him or her. If necessary, follow up with a grounding by dropping your hands to your sides in dola mudra and establishing that same breathing connection pattern while focusing on your connection and energy exchange with the earth.

Drawing Power from the Sun

This meditation will give you a powerful boost of energy, as if you had eaten a nutritious meal, but without weighing you down. The sun is the ultimate source of all life on earth. Symbolically, the sun is the source of all self-regeneration, self-sustaining health, and balance. Drawing Power from the Sun can help you get in touch with the divine masculine as well as boost your own healing. Draw power from the sun if you need to jump-start your success in any area of life or to aid natural healing and a sense of wellness. I use this ritual before going for a long run instead of eating a heavy meal. Sometimes, I use this ritual in the middle of the day if I feel an afternoon slump of energy. This little daytime ritual is a perfect excuse for me to take a break from work and take a step outdoors.

Drawing Power from the Sun can also be used daily, or even multiple times a day, in conjunction with other healthy weight-loss measures to suppress appetite and gain energy. This meditation is so powerful that this paragraph is all about safety cautions. Of course, meditation is a complementary therapy and not something to be used instead of a doctor's treatment if being underweight or overweight is a medical issue for you. This meditation must be performed during the day because it requires that sunlight be shining on the air that you breathe. Note that it is okay if you are wearing sunblock or clothing that blocks the sun, and this meditation works even in dappled sunlight, on overcast days, or indoors at a window. Never increase your risk of skin cancer for the benefit of meditation. Even though this meditation ritualistically honors the sun, it is all about deep breathing rather than physically being exposed directly to sunlight.

Begin by seating yourself outdoors or near a window. Place your hands on your head so that your thumbs gently cover your closed eyelids and your index fingers gently cover your ears. If you can, focus only on your breathing and any warmth of sunlight on your body. The placement of your hands is in token of sensory deprivation, mildly and symbolically removing sight and hearing from your perceptions so that your other senses are even more receptive to the spiritual energy being gathered. Take at least three deep breaths before intoning the following sun invocation. This works best if you memorize the invocation before the meditation so that you can keep your eyes covered with your thumbs. A nifty trick for those with memory issues is to record yourself reading the invocation ahead of time, leaving a pause after each line so that you can repeat it during the actual meditation by playing back the recording.

"Food of the Gods" Sun Invocation
Divine light, inner flame.
White of the sun; truth in a name.
Divine one within, my essence is power.
Integration will let harmony flower.
My soul commands, in tune it says:
I'm living on prana. So it is. So it is.

Next, you will form the nourisher (pushan) mudra with your hands for the remainder of the meditation. Your right hand will touch the middle finger and ring finger to your thumb and your left hand will touch the middle finger and index finger to your thumb. This meditation should last nine or nineteen minutes as a symbolic nod to the numerology of success and the sun. Ideally, this meditation should be performed after a period of spiritual fasting, but you can avoid a lengthy fast by simply performing this meditation before breakfast in the morning. Drawing power from the sun can also be part of a larger ritual. In the next chapter, more rituals will be explored.

Drawing Power from the Moon

Another common ritual component is the practice of Drawing Power from the Moon. You can draw power from the moon to boost healing, productivity, psychic sight, and magical power to bend your reality to conform with your desires. In this ancient practice, you will become close to the divine feminine. So powerful is this process that I recommend drawing power from the moon from a kneeling, sitting, or lying position since there is a potential for feeling light-headed and thus a fall risk. I know that it's a hassle to bring out a lawn chair for a meditation, particularly during the winter, but it's important to both be under a visible full moon and to be fully relaxed for the beginner to draw power from the moon.

Begin by grounding yourself. Grounding is a process of exchanging spiritual energy with the earth to achieve a calm but alert state of being. Begin by relaxing with your hands in dola, extended gently to your sides at an angle and hands drooping relaxed at the wrists. If you are seated or lying on the ground, your hands will naturally touch the ground, but it is okay if they do not if you are kneeling, squatting, or sitting on a chair. Take a moment to check in with your body and notice what areas feel tense. As you relax, try to see your internal energy pattern in your mind's eye. What does energy look like when it is flowing freely? What does energy look like when it is stuck? Some people visualize light or smoke.

Now, bring your attention to your connection with the earth. See your connection to the earth in your mind's eye. Some may visualize it as an anchor, a root, a cord, or some other structure. With every exhale you take, see in your mind's eye that any stuck or excess energy is flowing down through this connection harmlessly into the earth. Know that Mother Earth will reuse this energy wherever it is needed. With every inhale, see in your mind's eye that refreshing energy is being drawn from the earth into your body, suffusing every cell from your core to your fingertips. Ideally, this grounding part of the meditation should take about nine minutes, but it is okay if it is longer.

Now, fix your eyes upon the moon and form the moon altar mudra with both hands held parallel to each other's palms, the thumbs folded over at the first joint to form an altar when the hands are connected at the thumbs. Hold your hands up so that the moon appears to rest on this altar from your visual point of view. Take three deep breaths and then intone the following invocation without breaking your gaze.

"Change Manifestation" Moon Invocation
O, Moon!
Hail, bright moon of the seasons!
Guiding jewel, I give you my hands.
Grant hours of ease for every reason,
Myself and my kind throughout the lands.
Cast light into my soul.
Fair moon, may it be so.
I pray light up my mind.
As seasons come and seasons go.

When you have completed the invocation, blow two kisses to the moon, and then repeat the grounding meditation that proceeded the invocation, ideally for another nine minutes if possible and practical. The entire meditation for Drawing Power from the Moon should last approximately eighteen minutes but can certainly take longer if you wish, or it can be abbreviated as part of a longer ritual.

Receiving Psychic Messages from the Divine or the Departed

Automatic writing is the process of channeling messages from spirit; that is, your hand will do the writing but the divine will provide the content of the message. This automatic writing exercise is excellent for performing after Drawing Power from the Moon to receive psychic messages from the divine or after holding the yoni mudra to represent a portal between death and life, in order to speak with spirits of the dead. While meditating with the modern yoni mudra, be sure to fix your mind on the specific spirit you would wish to consult and speak or chant the name if you know it. Hold this priming meditation for ten to twenty minutes if possible before the automatic writing exercise. Some people believe that there should be some spiritual protection around you when you open a portal to the world of the dead, like a protective amulet or a projected circle of sacred energy. However, spirits are a natural occurrence in our world, and being afraid of the average spirit is very much like being afraid of the birds that come to your bird feeder. For most spirit communications, especially those with a loved one you will recognize, no extra protective measures need to be taken. Just talk with them!

After your yoni or Drawing Power from the Moon meditation, hold both your hands in hamsasya, which means you will touch your thumb to your index finger on each hand. Hold your nondominant hand to touch your thumb and index finger to your forehead, right between your eyes. Automatic writing can be done with the eyes open or closed. With your dominant hand, lightly hold a pen over a piece of paper. Hold this pose until the message comes. You may wish to focus on a question to ask of spirit, or you may just wish to sit in silent, receptive meditation. As soon as you sense the moment is right, grip the pen with your dominant hand and begin to write quickly, heedless of the words you may be writing. You may choose to use your usual grip on the pen or to grip it in the shikhara mudra, holding your dominant hand in the thumbs-up pose but with the pen wrapped by your fingers. You will naturally sacrifice some legibility, so the beginner may wish to start by simplifying this exercise with the usual grip.

When you have completed the writing and the urge to write subsides, form the kangula mudra (or padmakosha for a simpler mudra). Hold each hand palm down and point your fingertips and thumbs downward. Now curl your ring fingers into your palms and flick your wrists as if you were ringing bells while you thank the spirits and say goodbye. This polite banishing releases them from you and your home. Take a moment to read your message from spirit. If it is illegible, keep practicing. If the message doesn't make sense, write the date down and review it later to see if it makes more sense.

Malevolent Mudras and How to Counteract Them

In everyday life, that mean secretary at work might not secretly be an evil witch who mutters curses while fluttering her hands over your handwriting. However, there absolutely are harmful gestures that can boost magic of ill intent, just as there are effective mudras for empowering your positive spiritual works. In my book *Have You Been Hexed?* I explained the nature of how hexes are placed. Many of my clients whose curses I have broken had their curse placed while traveling to countries in which hexes are commonplace. There aren't evil witches stalking around, like in the movies. There are many people in this world for whom magic is a weapon of defense from perceived dangerous people, like us foreigners. Curses can also be a way to reclaim a sense of honor after a perceived wrong. Not all places in this world have lawful and trusted police forces, leaving people with nothing to resort to but their old traditions. Before learning how to protect yourself, it's important to be knowledgeable about what type of curse is being laid upon you so that you can choose the most effective defense. Here are the two most common types of malevolent magic that you are likely to encounter.

The Evil Eye

By far, the most common curse the world over since the beginning of time is what is called the "evil eye." The evil eye is not always performed with mudras but often is. In its simplest form, the evil eye is an intense glare with malevolent intentions. I'm sure that each of us can remember a person who could nearly bring a person to his or her knees with furious eye contact. Many people are trained, or are born with a natural gift, for an off-putting gaze that can cause real discomfort. However, a glare alone is not always enough to cast an effective and lasting curse; otherwise all children would have more reason to fear their mothers! A true evil eye is always done intentionally and often accompanied by mudras, magic words, or both.

The important thing to know about hexes like the evil eye, especially when traveling among people or regions where curses are commonplace, is that they are not cast for no reason at all. You don't have to worry when traveling, as long as you don't make a fool of yourself. Hexes are simply another weapon of defense or revenge. If a person would not lay physical hands on you, that person would not curse you either. However, if someone perceives that you are financially ripping them off or being rude or inappropriate to a loved one, you may be targeted.

Psychic Vampires

Psychic vampirism is a name given to a very real behavior that is only metaphorically related to its blood-sucking namesake. A psychic vampire interacts with the spiritual energy signatures of other people. Your body is surrounded by spiritual energy all the time, which flows to heal you and support your spiritual goals that you wish to manifest. Some people can perceive this energy visually, as auras. Psychic vampires are normal people who, either consciously or unconsciously, are drawn to syphon off the energy of others to support their own systems. Not every psychic vampire is intentionally a negative person. You might even be friends with a psychic vampire. If you have ever felt unusually drained after an ordinary interaction with someone, it is possible that you have been a victim of psychic vampirism.

Encountering a psychic vampire is not usually physically or spiritually dangerous and is more often a minor annoyance that fades on its own within hours. Symptoms can include fatigue, headache, irritability, negative thoughts, overwhelm, nausea, extreme sensitivity, dizziness, tremor, weakness, and inability to concentrate. A bigger danger of psychic vampirism is a daily or near constant assault. You may have a coworker or family member who is unwittingly draining you. With so few breaks to naturally replenish yourself, you might find yourself unable to meditate or get any work done. Psychic vampires don't even have to use magic words or gestures to affect you. They may simply be putting extra effort into making physical contact. Or they might find it fun to invade your personal space and share your energy.

Some psychic vampires are good people. Children, for example, are usually natural psychic vampires as they work on developing their own internal spiritual energy pattern by imprinting on those of the adults around them. There may be a high turnover in professionals who work with children because many enter the profession without any natural protection against the draining job of being around so many energetically needy little beings. A regular grounding meditation practice can help you inoculate yourself against the everyday psychic vampire, and the protective mudras described in this chapter will help in a pinch.

How to Recognize Curse Mudras

The following mudras can be used to curse when held in specific positions toward a person who is in direct line of sight of the person casting the spell. Note that the mudras in and of themselves are by no means evil. You may have used each of them so far, if you've been following along with the exercises in this book. That is why I make a distinction with each of their forms by calling them by a different name.

Suchi as Pointing

The oldest and most common curse gesture is simply the pointed finger. Pointing at a person is considered rude partly because of its ancient associations with hex magic. A person using this mudra to hex will be pointing directly at you while using the evil eye gaze. Words may be spoken aloud or not when casting the evil eye with a pointed finger.

Hamsasya as Poison in God

Hamsasya is usually the OK sign in Western culture, but it can be used to cast a curse. A person using this mudra to hex will gesture with it directly at their target while speaking nasty words. This mudra's curse is only used in conjunction with words.

Sign of the Horns as Corna

The sign of the horns can be used to either hex or to heal. When used to hex, a person will always point the horns—that is, the little finger and index finger—directly toward the target, often with a waggle at the wrist. Hexes might be cast with or without accompanying magic words with this mudra.

Travel Protection Mudras to Counter the Evil Eye

The evil eye is often countered through the use of talismans. Around the world, mirrors are the most common talisman against the evil eye, with the idea that the negative energy will be reflected back to the caster. There are many, usually blue, eyelike charms that are sold to protect against the evil eye. The first three of the countering mudras that follow are so effective that they are often made into talismans. A small model of a hand forming the mudra is hung on a cord around the neck. Luckily, even if you don't own such a talisman, you have the means to make the mudra with your own hands. Make note that most hex-breaking mudras are considered rude and so should be done surreptitiously, such as behind the back or in a pocket. Even if the gesture itself isn't obscene, it's usually not very nice to directly imply that somebody is casting a hex on you. It might escalate conflicts. Few protective mudras are required to be used in direct line of sight with the attacker, even though the curses themselves require this. In the protective exercises that follow, the requirements for the mudras to be visible will be noted if required. More context will be added later in the chapter with specific exercises for some of the strongest mudras.

Mano Fico

The most common hex-breaking mudra, due to its effectiveness against all sorts and intensity of curses, is the mano fico, the fig gesture. Made as a fist with the thumb sticking through the index and middle fingers, the gesture can be perceived as the rudest gesture in this hex-breaking list, so take extra caution with its use and keep it hidden if possible.

Azabache

A notable exception to the rule, the azabache gesture is not considered rude. Its name refers to the glittering black gemstone known as jet, which also is believed to have protective magical properties. Make this sign by forming a fist and then pushing your index finger knuckle forward to allow it to protrude noticeably. The azabache mudra looks very similar to the kapitta mudra and can be used interchangeably with it due to natural variations in hand flexibility. This mudra is considered safe and appropriate for use on infants, by touching or gesturing toward the child, for protection.

Sign of the Horns

Since the sign of the horns can be used to hex, it is only logical that it can also be used to heal. To counter a hex with the sign of the horns, you need not direct the mudra at your attacker. If you are with people who might consider this gesture rude, remember to use it discreetly.

Hamsa: Talk to the Hand

An open palm pressed outward is an intuitive "stop" gesture. The open right hand with an eye in the center (hamsa) is often made into a talisman to hang or wear to ward off curses. I have a friend who even got an eye tattooed on each palm to ward away evil. You don't need to go as far as a tattoo, but an eye drawn with marker can be useful in hex-breaking rituals. Never underestimate your personal power to block energy being sent at you by simply raising a firm hand against it.

Sign of the Cross and Kartarimukha to Counter the Evil Eye

This ritual can be done on the spot if you have had the evil eye cast on you or as part of a larger ritual to remove a lasting curse. If done in person, this quick ritual will require line of sight and potentially quite a bit of bravery. Begin using your right hand. Touch your pointer and middle fingers to your thumb and keep your ring and pinkie fingers curled into your palm. Touch your body at your forehead, chest, right shoulder, and then left shoulder. Next, form kartarimukha by extending your pointer and middle fingers while curling the rest in a fist. Point the two fingers directly at the hex caster or at an image of the hex caster if done later in ritual. This gesture might look a little bit like if you were a parent gesturing to your eyes and then to a child to tell him or her, "I've got my eyes on you."

Padmakosha

Pushing your fingers outward, away from your palm, makes your hand form a shape that looks like a bell. Take care not to make a claw hand, although that defensive gesture can scare away evil enough! Bells are used to drive out negativity by filling the space with beautiful sound. A metaphorical bell made with your hand can be shaken in lieu of a bell. Since this gesture is not insulting, it can be used in plain sight, though it need not be.

Crossed Fingers

Crossing the fingers is a commonplace gesture in Western culture that may have Christian origins. A multipurpose sign for luck, protection, and permission for little white lies, there are some unfortunate rude connotations to crossed fingers meaning female genitals as an insult. Consider discretion when using crossed fingers openly, especially during travel. Hide your crossed fingers by default since we do live in a multicultural society.

Swastikam for Hex Blocking

Another firm gesture, similar to the palm outward, is to make flat palms and then cross your wrists in front of you as if to say no with confidence. This gesture is not very subtle but has clear intention. It is best used in situations in which standing up for yourself is called for.

Shakatam for Hex Blocking

Just as bells scare away negative energy, so do masks or scary faces. The scary face that can be used in ritual to block negative energy from any direction is shakatam, which resembles a demon with large teeth. Curl your index fingertip into the space between your index finger and thumb to make the large canine teeth with each hand, and then hold your hands to either side of your face with wide eyes to complete the effect. This one would be awkward to make in person, but ritual uses will be described in this chapter.

The "No" Mudra

A meditative mudra that is excellent for removing negative energy from your person or space is the "no" mudra, made by linking your hands together as if a chain with your index finger touching the thumb on each hand, and then tenting the remaining fingers. This one is obvious to use but not very recognizable by others who are not also experts on the mudras.

Sometimes You Are Your Own Worst Enemy

More often than not, people who experience the effects of a curse in their lives are powerful people who have accidentally used their own personal power to hex themselves. If you are like many of my clients who have requested hex breaking, you might have noticed an unbelievable pattern of negativity in your life. An unlikely string of misfortunes can lead you to believe that nothing in your life can go right, which compounds the effects of this spiritual trap. Before I describe rituals that can destroy any curse placed on you by another person at any point in your life or ancestry, it is important that you learn the techniques to control your own power. In some ways, the following exercises may feel therapeutic, but they are of course no substitute for therapy from a professional if you are dealing with the accumulated trauma of extremely unfortunate life circumstances.

Self-Binding with the Patience Mudra

In my fortune-telling work, I can honestly say that more than half of my clients already knew the answers to their problems before they walked into the room with me. Most were merely looking for confirmation from an outside spiritual perspective. They knew full well that they could get their own internal spiritual perspective for free at home. But it helped them gain more confidence in their life choices if they heard from someone like me that things could work out if they just stayed the course. They felt at peace when told to wait and keep working the boring job until finishing school, or to wait for a better job to come along. They relaxed a bit with the knowledge that their relationship was still developing and that they shouldn't rush into marriage. Unfortunately, there were a lot of impatient people too. People who were frustrated with me because I wouldn't tell them the answers that they wanted to hear, usually answers that required no patience at all. They wanted to be told to drop everything and move across the country to be with a new boyfriend, or to fire a long-time employee before giving her time and training to improve.

Chances are, there are some things in your own life that you know need real patience, the type of calm restraint that is excruciating to endure. If you cut corners or push ahead too early, you know that the outcome will not be ideal. Now, imagine somebody else was meddling with your life by pushing too hard, urging you to charge ahead. You would want to restrict or restrain that person. Through practical means, that might mean cutting down on communications with that pushy person. But since you can't very well restrict communication with yourself, a spiritual practice called a binding is recommended. Binding is a magical method that you can use to restrain yourself with your own willpower.

This binding work recommends some extra tools, but you can omit them if desired. The supplies you'll want are a very small piece of paper with a representation of yourself. This can be a photo or a slip of paper with your name on it, and some string in black, red, or white. Begin the exercise by seating yourself and conjuring up an image in your mind of the outcome you would like to achieve through your patience. For example, if you are trying to persevere with your studies so that you won't quit school, visualize yourself at graduation wearing the cap and gown. When you have the image you need strongly in your mind, wrap the string around the picture or your name until the image or letters are completely hidden by string.

When you have completed the wrapping, place the small piece of paper in the palm of your left hand, then form the patience mudra by curling your fingers and then hooking the curled fingers of your right hand into your left hand and pressing your right hand's knuckles down on the piece of paper. Commence meditation, holding the image in your mind of your success. While you meditate, try to keep tension on your hands by allowing them to pull against each other. Hold this tension as long as you are physically able to. It is okay if your arms shake while your muscles work. When you have completed this meditation, keep the wrapped piece of paper somewhere safe, ideally in a box filled with salt. If you choose to undo the binding early, you can unwrap it. When you have successfully completed your goal, you can burn it or bury it if the materials are biodegradable.

Meditation of Unsending

I have had many people come to me believing that they may have a malevolent person in their life who is actively sending bad energy. Perhaps the person is an ex-girlfriend with a penchant for magic or an aunt who never approved of the person's choices and who consistently throws negativity and hate into his or her life. Here's what you can do when you essentially catch a negative person in the act. If you know that somebody out there is at home stewing about you and spitting venom your way, there are a couple of things that you can do to protect yourself. Remember the childhood phrase that was to be said when a bully called you names: "I am rubber and you are glue, whatever you say bounces off me and sticks to you." Here's the grown-up version.

If the perceived spiritual attack occurs in person, you can immediately block and counter it using one of the protective mudras in the section called "Travel Protection Mudras to Counter the Evil Eye" on page 158. They work on people close to you just as well as they work on strangers. It can help to take a deep breath and blow it out slowly while producing the protective mudra. If you are not in the presence of the person you believe is sending you negative energy, use this Meditation of Unsending instead.

Prepare for a meditation that can be done seated, standing, or lying down. It is advisable to find some privacy and preferably perform this meditation when nobody is home. The reason for solitude, if possible, is that you can more easily push any negative energy away from you in any direction without worrying about others. If others are nearby, however, one should just be more mindful to push any negative energy down into the earth. Energy can travel through any materials to reach the earth. Even if you're on the top floor of an apartment building, that energy will snake down through the walls, flooring, and foundation to find the earth if you set your intention to it.

To begin your meditation, form both hands into the mano fico, or the fig mudra, by making a fist with your thumb poking out between your index and middle fingers. Then, cross your arms at your wrists and press them against your chest. If you choose to add a mirror to this working, you can press it to your chest with your arms with the mirror facing out. The use of a mirror in many hex-stopping practices is to symbolically reflect any harmful energy. You can see the use of mirrors for protection in feng shui, a geomancy practice that involves mirrors and other decorative tools to alter the flow of energy in a space. If you don't have a suitable mirror, however, this exercise can be done without it since you'll be creating a sort of mirror in your mind's eye. The mirror, in this case, will surround you entirely as an energetic shield.

Close your eyes and allow yourself to sense your natural, internal energy pattern if you can. For some people, this is seen as a light or a color. For others, it is sensed as warm or chill air or a sense of static electricity that buzzes or crackles. If you are able to sense your internal energy pattern, strengthen and intensify it in your mind until it creates a firm wall around you. If you are not able to sense your own energy pattern, you can use visualization to see a shield around you in your mind's eye in whatever form feels strong and protective to you. A shield can be a bubble, a ring of fire, a halo, a box, a wall, or even a pack of animals.

As soon as you have your shield firm in your mind, take a deep breath and, as you breathe out, allow the mudra formation to push any negative energy out of your body into the earth. Those of you who are more sensitive may "see" the negative energy in a form such as darkness or smoke. Focus on deep breathing and keeping your focus on strengthening your own shield and internal energy pattern. Don't worry about your shield keeping any negative energy in. Your energy shield is semipermeable and will allow any harmful energy to disperse harmlessly while retaining the energy you need. Remember to establish your connection with the earth so that you are exchanging energy and not just depleting your own. With each breath in, pull fresh, rejuvenating energy back into your body. When you sense that the process of expelling negative energy is complete, spend a few extra breaths on grounding before you finish your meditation. This meditation can be repeated as necessary, but it is advisable to follow this meditation with the Lesser Banishing Ritual of the Pentagram on page 142 so that much of the work is being done for you by an energetic structure that you need only set up once in your home.

Cancel and Recall Hatred

You may have, at some point in your life, actually cast a magic curse on somebody. Recall that the evil eye, in its most mild form, is basically just an angry glare. Even though most of the readers who picked up this book are kind and gentle souls, it is unlikely that you've gotten this far in life without wishing ill upon someone while staring them down. In many faith traditions, it is thought that those who cast curses will experience spiritual consequences that can range from a bad headache to the wrath of the divine. Luckily, there are ways to undo hexes.

If you catch yourself in the act of hating someone, casting the evil eye on them, or otherwise losing control of your emotions and potentially harming another person, immediately start with the keep it together mudra. Pinch your index finger to your thumb on each hand and then hold the pinched hands together, tenting the rest of the fingers. Using a peaceful mudra stabilizes your energy as well as occupying your hands so that you can't amplify any negative magical or physical act with them. Remove yourself from the situation to stabilize your emotional thinking before trying to reverse or rectify the problem. If appropriate, consider using the Angry Argument Meditation on page 90 at this time.

The process of recalling and ending the curse may be surprisingly simple. Begin by grounding yourself and making sure that you have established a connection with the earth that flows back and forth with each breath. You will take a deep breath and, as you blow out, draw a simple sigil. Face north and draw the earth banishing pentagram with the pointed finger (suchi mudra) of your dominant hand while keeping your nondominant hand relaxed in dola mudra down toward the earth. Recall from chapter 3 that the earth banishing pentagram begins at the bottom left corner of the star and that you should redraw the last line so that you will end the sigil drawing by flicking your hand up to the sky to touch the top point of the star. The tricky part of this process is that you should attempt to continue simultaneously grounding yourself so that the negative energy you are banishing flows into the earth.

The final, important piece of the magic to recall and destroy the curse that you've attempted (possibly inadvertently) to throw is to spend a few minutes paying attention to your internal energy pattern. If you feel jittery or exhausted or if you sense that energy in your body is stuck, clouded, or dark, continue grounding until that feeling is eliminated. If you sense an ongoing negative connection to the person that you targeted, consider proceeding to a cord-cutting exercise. However, if you feel that your body, mind, and spirit are at peace, your work here is done.

Ritual of Uncrossing

Many people come to believe that a curse has already been placed upon them due to observing a history of unlikely misfortunes, hearing a family story about a curse, or the attacker bragging about placing the hex. Removing an ongoing hex or curse that you believe has been placed upon you or your family line needs little more than prayer. However, there are some preparatory measures that can be done in order to help you emotionally recover.

Prepare your space for the curse removal by, at a minimum, making sure that you have privacy and will not be interrupted. As with the Meditation of Unsending, you may wish to have an empty home, if possible. As in the exercise for Cleansing Your Life of a Codependent Toxic Person on page 192, it is also appropriate to bathe or shower yourself using the mrigashirsa mudra ahead of this ritual. When you dress yourself, take care not to wear anything with knots tied: for example, shoelaces or a drawstring. Open any windows and doors that are practical to invite fresh air into the space. Next, pray to ask for any negative energy to be removed. As you pray, hold the "no" mudra by creating links with your index fingers and thumbs to link the two hands together as if creating a chain. Allow the rest of your fingers to tent and touch. If you are new to prayer or feeling a little rusty, here's a simple prayer format that I like to teach by remembering the acronym PRAYING.

Person listening	Hail, (your god(s)/goddess(es)/spirit/universe/ higher self/etc.).
Raise praise	You who are (list three positive attributes), I praise you!
Ask for help	Thank you for removing any hex or negative energy from (full name).
Your deadline	Now.
Imperatives for safety	With harm to none and for the highest good of all. So may it be.
Note of thanks	In return, I offer you (gratitude/love and devotion/other offering).
Gracious attention	Blessed be.

At the end of your prayer, the gracious attention is important, because you will have an opportunity to look for signs that you are now free of the negativity that has been spiritually afflicting you. Spend a few breaths holding the self-acceptance, or love, mudra by putting your hands in a prayer pose and then curling the finger of your right hand over the curled finger of your left hand. Establish your connection with the earth to ground any excess energy and replenish yourself after any energy expenditure you've done during this process. This can be an excellent opportunity to journal about your experiences and feelings so that you can return to this moment of relief any time that natural misfortune strikes your life again. If you do feel any lingering connection with your attacker, you can perform the exercise for Cleansing Your Life of a Codependent Toxic Person on page 192.

Protection of an Infant, Pet, or Other Loved Ones

A simple blessing of protection against malevolent magic, often called a warding, can be done using the azabache (kapitta) mudra. Form your hand into a fist and then push the knuckle of your index finger forward. For some, this may be easier to do by wrapping the index finger around the tip of the thumb to push it forward. When standing in front of the person or pet you would like to ward (or a photo if not physically present), use the mudra with your dominant hand. Kiss the first knuckle of your thumb and then draw either a cross or an earth banishing pentagram over the person, pet, or photo. Remember that the earth banishing pentagram begins at the lower left-hand point and ends at the top point after you have redrawn the first line a second time at the end.

~ 5 ~
Protection

Most of this book is focused on self-help and solo practice, but mudras are an important way to move and share energy. Hands are communicative symbols that have power when connecting others with your intentions. If our personal energy aura surrounding our body were a wall socket to powerful energy, hands would be the way to plug in to someone else's energy. That may sound intrusive, but every conversation is a give-and-take. Entire languages can be spoken with the mere moving of hands in air, and entire dialogues can be shared with a mere touch. So many seek blessings every day from the simple image of an ardhapataka or tripataka mudra in a statue of a god or an image of a saint. Now you know what some of them mean. This chapter will be about sharing your newfound mudra power with others. With other forms of magic, you would need permission from others before doing something that affects them. If you were going to burn a lock of someone's hair in a love spell, it would be a good idea to get permission ahead of time. But mudras as blessings are like an extended hand for a handshake. You're asking, "Would you like to accept these energies?" If you don't believe me, here are some secular hand gestures that you use in everyday life that can be considered mudras.

Unique Signs of Greeting and Blessing

It would be cool if spiritual people really did signal to each other with the sign of the Goddess and sign of the God to indicate that they were kindred spirits. Unfortunately, this is not yet a widespread practice. Nevertheless, there are ways that you can use your hands to bless others during prayers or give well wishes. Here are a few mudras that I have seen used, and have used myself, during special occasions with friends and family.

The Triangle Mudra: In chapter 3 you learned that you could form a triangle with your hands and then gaze through it at a candle flame to infuse it with your intentions. You also learned that the triangle mudra can be done partnered, with each person holding one half of the triangle. This versatile mudra can also be used to bless others by holding up the triangle and gazing at the person just as you would the candle.

Ardhapataka or Tripataka: A simple and subtle blessing is your hand raised in ardhapataka, which is formed by making a flat palm and then bending your pinkie and ring fingers at a 90-degree angle, or as close to it as your body allows. A variant of tripataka, in which three fingers are held up but pressed together, is used as a salute and to swear oaths.

Kapotam: This mudra is made by first forming prayer hands and then tenting your hands while keeping your thumbs together, to create a pocket of air between your palms. This mudra can be used in greeting as a sign of respect. It represents respectful conversations, acceptance, and obedience.

Dinner Invocation

I'd like to share some dinner invocation mudras that I use with my own family every full moon, but it is suitable for daily use. It requires only two simple mudras, ardhachandra and suchi. Suchi is merely the pointed finger, and ardhachandra is the flat hand with thumb extended outward, as if you were extending your hand for a handshake with fingers pressed together. You can use these mudras wordlessly or with words. In the following example, I will base the words on the prayer format that was taught on page 167 in the "Ritual of Uncrossing" section.

For the first part of this family ritual, everyone will be mirroring the leader, but the mirroring will not be done slowly. Begin the blessing by having everyone extend hands high and outward in ardhachandra, addressing the sky overhead. The leader should say:

LEADER: Hail, (your god(s)/goddess(es)/spirit/universe/higher self/etc.). You who are in everything above us."

The leader extends hands in ardhachandra directly out to the sides and everyone follows.

LEADER: You who are here in our home.

The leader places hands in ardhachandra over his or her heart, and everyone follows. This is the last movement that the entire family must follow from the leader.

LEADER: You who are here in our hearts. I praise you! Thank you for the blessing of this feast tonight. May it give us energy for our goals, with harm to none, and for the highest good of all. So may it be.

The leader alone makes a banishing pentagram with suchi mudra over the food at the table. That is, the leader uses the pointer finger to draw a star starting from the bottom left corner and finishing by redrawing the first line again and ending at the top of the pentagram. The leader then puts a tiny portion of each food at the table on a small offering plate.

LEADER: In return, I offer you this share of our meal. Blessed be.

There should be a period of silence, save for the passing of food with the blessing "May you never hunger." After the meal, the offering should be placed outside for the birds and squirrels to be proxies for the divine consuming your offering. Be sure that your offering ingredient amounts are not harmful to wildlife.

Spirit of Place Blessing

Acknowledging land and the spirit of place at the location of a wedding, ritual, or meeting has two purposes. One is a spiritual purpose. Our world is filled with spiritual fauna, some of whom may interact with us on a regular basis and some of whom may keep to themselves. It is polite to acknowledge the powerful forces and entities that exist on the land where you stand. Another purpose is a social justice purpose. Many of the homes and venues in which you may be sitting were once walked by indigenous people, most of whom were forcibly removed from the land on which they live. With a little research, you may be able to find out what indigenous territories surround you.

There are only three mudras, but many movements, involved in this blessing. The mudras that you will be using are ardhapataka, pataka, and dola. Pataka is the flat palm with fingers and thumb pressed together, and ardhapataka is just like pataka except that the ring and pinkie fingers are bent over at a roughly 90-degree angle, or whatever your body allows. Both offer blessings, but while pataka radiates them out everywhere, ardhapataka directs the blessings in specific directions, which is important when we're acknowledging the cardinal directions in a space. Dola aids in grounding and recognizing the earth below and is done by lowering arms to the sides a little bit away from the body and allowing the hands to relax downward. The arm and body movements for this blessing take four steps to complete, but the first one is a doozy since you'll be drawing a circle in a similar manner as the circle casting in the Greater Universal Rite of Worship and Magic you were introduced to in chapter 3. Be gentle with yourself and carry this book into ritual as a cheat sheet if you need it. This is more complex stuff, but if you've been practicing along in previous chapters, you're ready for it.

Step 1: Drawing a Circle

Face to the north. Form ardhapataka mudra by extending two fingers and point it directly to the north. Say,

Spirit of place, you are here. In the silence of rocks and when the earth speaks with the crunch of sand beneath feet.

Slowly turn your body with ardhapataka extended in front of you so that you are facing northeast. Say,

Spirit of place, you are here. In the gentle dance of dry leaves and the tornado's defiant strength.

Slowly turn your body with ardhapataka extended to complete the semi-circle you've drawn and face east. Say,

Spirit of place, you are here. In the breeze that delights and causes faces to turn to the wind in reverie, and in the startling gust that clears the mind and brings one into the present moment.

Slowly turn your body with ardhapataka to face southeast. Say,

Spirit of place, you are here. In the dry desert wind bringing relief to the traveler and in the harsh gale feeding the wildfire's devastating renewal.

Slowly turn your body with ardhapataka to face south. Say,

Spirit of place, you are here. In the fire of determination and the sun's warmth that lights up summer memories.

Slowly turn your body with ardhapataka to face southwest. Say,

Spirit of place, you are here. In the curative power of hot springs and the steaming blast of an ancient geyser.

Slowly turn your body with ardhapataka to face west. Say,

Spirit of place, you are here. In the silent pond that is the frog's womb. In the wisdom of a murmuring creek and a spring rain. In the ocean's world of life.

Slowly turn your body with ardhapataka to face northwest. Say,

Spirit of place, you are here. In the glaciers watching us from rocky peaks and the aftermath of the flooded valley, where long-dormant seeds awaken.

Complete drawing the circle with ardhapataka by turning your body north.

Step 2: Cross the Circle

From your position, facing north with ardhapataka extended, raise your arm over your head and turn the opposite direction to face south, bringing your arm down to complete the arc, and point directly south with ardhapataka. Say,

Spirit of place, you are here. In magma stirring since Earth's birth.

Turn to face east. With ardhapataka extended, raise your arm over your head in an arc and turn your body to the opposite direction to face west and point ardhapataka directly west. Say,

Spirit of place, you are here. In rolling fog from the ocean's breath.

Step 3: Centering

Draw the entire circle clockwise once more with ardhapataka while saying,

Spirit of place, you are here. In leaf and bud, flower and fruit. In the crunch of dried leaves and the dance of snowflakes.

Change both hands to pataka mudra and raise them to the sky, saying,

Spirit of place, you are here in the grand dance of life. In fin and feather and bone.

Change mudra downward to dola and say,

Spirit of place, you are here. In the love of kindred we share here on Earth. You are present in each of us. You are welcome. You are welcome. You are welcome.

Step 4: Land Acknowledgment

With hands in pataka, raise your arms in front of you, elbows bent loosely, with palms facing your head.

I have arrived. I have arrived. I acknowledge that I live, learn, worship, and make magic on the sacred ancestral land of the native (insert names of Indigenous groups of the location if possible). All my relations.

Séance

A séance is a group meeting to attempt to commune with the spirits of the dead. A family séance can be a way to contact ancestors who have died. It is also okay to have a little fun with a séance with your friends, especially around Halloween. Some people believe that a séance is a dangerous portal to the other world, but those folks usually don't understand that the spirit world exists alongside us at all times and that there are all sorts of natural spirit interactions that occur on a regular basis between humans and ghosts. Is it not better to be mindful, intentional, and in control of such dealings? Here are complete instructions on how to safely conduct a séance with mudras. There are some tools that I suggest using to enhance the results of your séance. Here are the ingredients for a successful séance:

- A dark bowl, preferably black.
- The darkest cooking oil you can find. Sesame oil works great.
- A crystal, preferably a quartz sphere or, better yet, a quartz crystal skull.
- Plenty of your favourite incense. Frankincense works well.
- A candle or candles for lighting, preferably five black candles, although tealights are okay.
- Three to six cool friends; more is okay if you have a table that seats more.

The other good ingredient is timing. The best time for a séance is during a full moon. The best seasons for hosting a séance are end of April to early May and end of October to early November. Prepare for the séance by filling the dark bowl with oil and setting it in the center of the table along with the crystal and a candle. The optional four extra candles are to be placed at the four cardinal directions of the room.

You should boost the table candle's magic by dressing and blessing it. If you don't want to do this in front of your guests, you may prepare the candle beforehand. For optional added protection from anything spooky, you should also cast a circle and clear the space before the ceremony using the

Greater Universal Rite of Worship and Magic found on page 136. This needs to be done at the beginning, and while all the guests are present. Then begin the séance rituals.

First, bless the candle that you'll be placing in the center of the table. Here's a brief refresher. Dress the candle with oil. You can use the sesame oil with a bit of crushed incense like frankincense steeped in it. To apply the dressing oil to the candle, put a few drops of oil in your palms. Form your hands into chatura mudra by tucking the candle under the thumbs of each hand and lifting your pinkie finger. With this grasp, beginning at the middle of the candle, rub the oil onto the outside of the candle by twisting your hands in opposite directions and pulling them toward the opposite ends of the candle. With this gesture, you will have wiped some of the oil from your palms onto the candle. While you do so, you can focus on your intention to communicate with the dead. Here are some focus ideas:

- Chant the names of your deceased ancestors.
- Visualize a specific person whose spirit you would like to call to the table.
- Pray that you will act as a good channel through which the spirits may speak.

Next, light the candle in a safe candleholder. This doesn't have to be on the table yet. It might be on an altar or some other place of importance where you can supervise your candle's burn. With your pointer finger (suchi mudra), draw the fire invoking pentagram safely high enough above the burning candle flame that you don't singe your hands. Don't forget to trace the final line as a repeat of the first line, so that that one line is "drawn" twice. Immediately after drawing the pentagram, form both hands into chandrakala mudra, which is simply a flat hand with thumb sticking out perpendicular to the fingers. Gesture with the hands to pull the energy from the pentagram that you've drawn slowly down over the candle, at a safe distance of course, by drawing your hands down at the sides as if you're slowly putting a glass bell jar lid over the entire candle. If it isn't already there, place the candle now in the center of the table.

Everything is ready for a séance, whether you cast an elaborate circle and dressed the candle in front of your guests or simply ushered them in the door and invited them to sit down at a table with a lit candle, a bowl of oil, and a crystal. No matter how sophisticated your friends are, they'll need a briefing about what is about to happen. There's no reason to refrain from holding mudras during the talking portion of the program. Guide your guests to hold trishira mudra, which is a simple mudra made by tenting all one's fingers and thumbs. You, as leader, will hold a more complex mudra: the soul vibration mudra. It is formed by touching the first knuckle of your last three fingers while touching the tips of your index fingers and the tips of your thumbs.

Explain that the trishira mudra they are holding represents activating the spiritual energy pathways of the body and will allow the spiritual energy to be passed along flawlessly around the people sitting at the table. Point out that you are using a different mudra, which will help shout your own soul's vibration into the universe to properly request a response from the spirit realm. Basically, the earth is the battery, your friends are the wires, and you are the light bulb. Explain that you will be using gestures to symbolically take the spiritual energy inside of yourself from spirit. Channeling means that you'll be connecting those imaginary wires to the spirit world to act as their light bulb too. Ask your guests to speak out the names of any deceased loved ones they would like to hear from, and tell everyone to get ready to silently meditate and be receptive for any response. Give them the final instruction that when you place your hands flat on the table, everyone at the table should place their hands flat on the table, with fingers splayed, and push their hands toward the center of the table until they touch pinkie fingers with the person next to them. The connection of hands at pinkie fingers around the table should be maintained by guests throughout the séance, unless someone feels a need to quietly excuse him- or herself.

Next, form your hands into hamsasya by touching your thumb and index fingers together. Hamsasya is a prana mudra that connects your energy to the crystal, that it may hopefully vibrate and reflect the energy of the spirits. Pick up the crystal and place it gently in the oil. Now, raise your hand slowly up in an arc over your head and change the mudra to arala. The arala mudra is just a flat hand with the pointer finger bent. Lower arala slowly down to your face and then tip your hand as if you are drinking a beverage to symbolically drink in energy and become a channeling conduit for messages from beyond. Now is the time to flatten your own hands on the table with fingers splayed and connect with the group that should be copying you to create a circle of energy around the table.

The rest is up to divine will and the personalities of the spirits that you've invited to the table. Everyone need only breathe deep breaths and wait in silent and receptive meditation. You, as the leader of the séance and the main channel for communication, may sense a message from spirit in the form of an inner voice, vision, physical sensation, breakthrough thought, or other phenomenon. To show that you will now speak a message, remove your hands from the circle of hands and make shakatam mudra at your face. This is a graceful motion that not only draws silent attention to the message you are about to share, but also works to frighten away any nasty entities from any other planes of existence. To form shakatam, bring your hands to the sides of your face and draw them slightly away from your cheeks while curling the tip of your pointer fingers into the webbing of your thumbs and touching the pads of your middle fingers to your thumbs. Speak what you may, and then place your hands back on the table and reconnect the circle of hands if you would like to wait for more messages or ask for clarification from the spirit.

When the séance is complete, thank any spirits that were present, named or unnamed, silent or eloquent, and then pull your hands away from the circle of hands to snuff the candle. Take a moment to discuss the séance with your guests, as some may have had their own perceptions of messages that they either received directly or heard from you. It is a good idea to share a meal or a snack of salty foods to help with grounding, since many of the participants may never have successfully done a grounding meditation before. Don't forget to close the circle before any guests leave if you used the circle casting from chapter 4.

Handfasting

Congratulations on your engagement! A wedding is a highly personalized marriage ceremony with a binding legal result. A handfasting can be done in addition to, or instead of, a wedding and may or may not be legally binding, depending on your preference. I have officiated many handfastings and had one of my own. This example of a handfasting ceremony is really just a chronological way for me to present some modular building blocks. Very few people will be able to follow this ceremony to the letter since, for example, one can't guarantee that one's officiant is willing to learn mudras as an added value service. Don't worry—any mudras suggested for guests will be simple to both explain and perform. I will also omit prescribing specific vows or other words for handfasting, since experience has shown me that most couples who desire an alternative ceremony to a wedding want to write their own words that frame their faith tradition and distinctive relationship together.

Before the main ceremony begins, many couples choose to create sacred space at the venue. It is possible to use the Greater Universal Rite of Worship and Magic from on page 136, but a logistical issue is that the circle casting is meant to keep good energy in and bad energy out, which means that one should avoid having guests enter or leave the circle once it is up. Going back and forth through the sacred boundaries you've set undermines the integrity of the bubble in which you're trying to gather and concentrate the loving energy in the room or space. A second logistical issue is that the giant circle casting will add to the length of the handfasting ceremony, which many couples want to keep short and sweet. A workaround to both of these problems is to cast the circle before the guests enter the room or space, and then have someone be in charge of opening and closing an invisible "gate" at the circle boundary.

For this to work, you'll need to have a waiting area as the guests arrive. After the circle is cast, the gatekeeper then uses ardhapataka mudra (two fingers extended) to cut a triangular hole in the cast circle boundary big enough for the guests to easily walk through. It can be a nice added touch for the gatekeeper to say a blessing to each guest as they pass through. Recall that ardhapataka mudra can be done with the palm facing toward each guest to bless him or her. You may also use the triangle mudra by forming a triangle with your index fingers touching and thumbs touching and then looking through it at each guest to frame his or her face. After all the guests pass through, the gatekeeper can seal up the gate by retracing the triangle with the mudra. It is best to cast an enormous circle that encompasses the washrooms of the venue so that your poor gatekeeper isn't busy throughout the ceremony gating people in and out.

When all the guests have been seated and are waiting for the ceremony to begin, there will be an opportunity for the guests to hold the wedding rings in a mudra and whisper their own personal good wishes to the couple into them. This works best if you use a long roll of string that can wind through the seating of the audience with the rings strung onto the string like beads. That way great-grandpa's trembling fingers won't drop the rings under his chair. Have the officiant or the usher explain the mudra. It also helps to have a picture of the mudra and an explanation of the ring blessing in the waiting area so that guests are prepared before they sit down. The guests should enfold the rings in the kapotam mudra. The kapotam mudra is made by first forming prayer hands and then tenting your hands while keeping your thumbs together, to create a pocket of air between your palms into which guests may whisper their personal blessings. The mudra represents respectful acceptance of the union and of the couple.

When the wedding party is ready for the ceremony to begin, the officiant has a number of mudras and movements that are excellent to use to affirm and bless the couple's union. Here are a few two-handed mudras that your officiant can hold during the ceremony. Note that they are all two-handed, so it helps if you've conscripted an officiant who can memorize their own lines in the ceremony so that they won't have to turn any pages.

Nagabandham to Bherunda: Use this movement as an opening or closing blessing for the couple. The nagabandham mudra symbolizes intertwined snakes, offering the blessing of a long life together. Bherunda mudra is a two-handed kapitta mudra and represents two lovebirds. To bless with the two together, begin the movement with hands crossed at the wrist. Use flat palms and curved first knuckles of all fingers and thumbs to show two serpent heads. Now, allow both hands to change to kapitta to form bherunda by forming a fist and then wrapping the index finger around the tip of the thumb. Next, pull the hands away from each other so that the two lovebirds face each other. This can be followed with a bow with hands in prayer pose (anjali).

Bliss: Hold the bliss mudra during the ceremony to radiate the blessing of a lifetime of following their bliss together. It looks like a heart shape. Touch the knuckles of your index fingers together, and you'll touch the knuckles of your middle and ring fingers to their counterparts as well. Your thumbs touch to form the point of the heart.

Love: This mudra celebrates the couple's passion for each other. Press the knuckles of just your middle fingers together and allow the rest of your fingers to tent, touching the thumbs in a downward position instead of upward with the rest of your fingers.

The "yes" mudra can absolutely be used by the couple to add an energetic exclamation point to the confirmation of the vows. However, most couples want to join both hands throughout the ceremony, which is impossible to do with this two-handed mudra, even if each side of the couple takes one half. Here is a reminder of the "yes" mudra in case you want to use it anyway. Touch the very tips of your thumbs to the inside of the first joint of your middle finger on each hand and hold both hands up facing each other with a small space between them. If desired, the couple can hold hands with one hand while sharing the formation of the "yes" mudra with the other.

Here are a few more mudras that a couple can share to hold hands throughout the ceremony. So that I can more accurately describe the act of sharing mudras, I'm going to call one partner the bride and the other the groom, though I acknowledge and celebrate the right of any gender combination to join together as a valid married couple.

Kurma: Since it feels much like the traditional clasping of hands, this mudra represents protection of the marriage and perseverance that the couple will use to stay together. There are two versions of sharing this mudra, so choose the one that feels most comfortable with your respective hand sizes. For one person, kurma is formed by extending your pinkie fingers, index fingers, and thumbs, and then clasping your hands together so that your middle fingers and ring fingers wrap around your hands. Note that the mudra should be oriented horizontally. It is sort of like making the "I love you" ASL sign into a sandwich. For the first way to share kurma, the groom should first form kurma, and the bride should enfold his kurma with her hands by placing the lower half of kurma below the groom's hands and wrapping the other half on top of his hands. The second version is done with the bride standing to the groom's right. He wraps his right arm around her waist and offers her the bottom half of kurma with his left hand, and she clasps his by completing the top half of kurma while her left arm is wrapped around his waist.

Self-Acceptance: Marriage is about accepting each other for life. It is important to accept your partner for who they are. It also helps if each of you learn to love yourselves before each other. To share the self-acceptance mudra, the bride should stand to the groom's right. He should wrap his right arm around her, and she should wrap her left arm around him. Each offers their free hand with a flat palm (pataka) and they should press their hands together. The groom should tuck his index finger down to frame his thumb, allowing the bride to wrap the tip of her index finger over his.

Inner Vision: The couple should share an inner vision for how life in their marriage will look, sound, and feel. The inner vision mudra is shared side by side with each partner having one arm around the other, as in the previous shared mudra. The partners should use their free hands to touch thumbs and interlace the knuckles of their pointer and middle fingers. The person on the right should have his or her index and middle fingers resting over the fingers of the other partner. The purpose of the inner vision mudra is to allow each other to see the truth, making it excellent for proving each other's love during vows.

Patience: Plenty of patience, for your partner and for yourself, is necessary to make any relationship work. The patience (Ganesh) mudra is the most subtle mudra to use among these, so it can be integrated secretly into even a traditional wedding. To share the patience mudra, the couple should face each other. Extend hands with left palm up and right palm down. The couple should clasp hands by curling their fingers around each other's fingers. Each should have their fingers fully tucked into the palm of the other. Bring your hands together so that the two instances of the patience mudra are pressed together, side by side. Both of you are committing to patience.

Unity Candle

It is an important part of many traditions to light a unity candle. That means that the couple will each use a lit candle of their own to light a shared, larger candle. Many mainstream weddings use colors that match the wedding's colors for style's sake, and that's okay. If you want to use symbolic colors, use a red candle for the unity candle. Red is the color of passion and deep love. It can be meaningful for each partner to choose a smaller candle of their favorite color, a color the person wears often, or one that is otherwise associated with his or her style or personality. Don't worry. Your personality is not being symbolically absorbed by the unity candle. All three candles will burn brightly at the end of the ceremony. However, to prepare to combine many parts of your life, all three candles will be dressed and blessed in the same way.

Dress the candles with grapeseed oil in which some rose petals have been steeped, or use petals of any flower that features most at your wedding. I suggest dressing the candles at the full moon before the ceremony, and saving the blessing of the candles for the actual event. That saves you from fumbling with oil during an already nerve-wracking performance in front of your friends and family. Each of you should dress your own personal candle by yourself, but both of you should take turns dressing the third unity candle. Feel free to use the same bottle of oil for all three.

Add a bit of the oil to your fingertips to dress the candles using padma-kosha mudra with both hands. The padmakosha mudra will bless your union with abundance. For those wanting to have a child, this mudra will add a special boost. To form padmakosha, hold your hands out palms up and then bend your fingers and thumbs skyward. Now you can dip your fingertips in oil. Dress the candle starting from the middle and twisting your hands in opposite directions while smearing the oil to either end of the candle. As you dress your candles together, both of you should focus on your shared intention for your marriage. You can talk together about it, rehearse your vows, or simply sit together in silent contemplation.

Remember to have candle holders for all three candles. You won't be using your personal candles as a mere match to light the unity candle. They need space to be blessed and space to burn down. Use chandrakala mudra to bless the candles, representing a new beginning. After lighting the personal candle and placing it in its holder, extend only your thumbs and pointer fingers of both hands horizontally, keeping the rest of your fingers curled into your palms. Frame the candle from a safe distance above and to either side of the flame and pull your fingers down to rest on the candleholders' platform. Practice this move ahead of time so that you can do it swiftly and deftly over your personal candle.

For the unity candle, each of you will first light it at the same time with your personal candles. Share the mudra by slowly, each of you, forming half of the mudra. Use your mirroring meditation skills to lower the mudra to the candleholders' platform in unison.

Wedding Toast Mudras

These one-handed mudras can be used, while lofting a glass, by members of the wedding party to bless the couple. If you are a guest at a wedding, feel free to throw in some mudras, as subtly or flamboyantly as your personal style. If you are somebody who talks with your hands, it is okay to move the mudra around in the air as you speak—and certainly preferable to spilling your champagne or mocktail all over your outfit by waving around the hand that holds the glass.

Alapadma: The most subtle mudra of this bunch, especially if you talk with your hands, alapadma is a graceful way to gesture. Representing the power and beauty of the lotus and the moon in its fullness, use this mudra to amplify the words you speak in toast. Hold your palm flat and splay the fingers with the pinkie and ring finger pointed upward and the rest directed as far back and downward as your body allows.

Kangula: A somewhat complex mudra to toast with is kangula. The mudra that symbolizes bells is appropriate to represent wedding bells at the toast. In one tradition of the Bharatanatyam dance form in which this mudra is used, actual ankle bells are often presented ceremonially from the teacher to the student, indicating pride. The bells are then treated as sacred when worn by the student. Use kangula especially if you are an older relative or mentor to one or both partners being wed. Hold your palm up with fingers and thumb also pointing upward, except the ring finger is curled to press its tip into the palm.

Katakaamukha: This mudra is held by Shiva's bride, Parvati, and is even more complex, but offers a powerful blessing with goddess energy as well as looking very graceful. Curl your index finger over your thumb and allow your middle finger to bend at a 90-degree angle while keeping your pinkie finger extended in line with your hand (the first form of katakaamukha). Your ring finger will naturally bend somewhere between the middle and pinkie as it is left extended. If you find this mudra tricky, return to page 21 to see guidance on how to transition between the two forms of katakaamukha.

Shield against Bad Vibes

Picture this: You're on a crowded commuter train in a foreign country and a particularly creepy individual stands quite close to you. He's not close enough to pickpocket you, but he's close enough that he is invading your personal space bubble, especially since the vibe that you get from him is negative, as if he's just looking for somebody with whom to pick a fight. There's a simple shield that you can make with the chakram mudra, which will extend your natural energetic shield to repel negative energy. This brief meditation can be done in public places and is also useful for creating inner calm if there are too many people around, for example, in a busy and over-crowded supermarket.

Everyone has a natural halo of spiritual energy that surrounds their body. Some people call this an aura. Your aura can be extended for many reasons. Perhaps you want to perform on stage and be noticed by a talent scout. Perhaps you want to reach out spiritually and connect with someone else. And, in this case, you want to sharpen the edges of that energy and extend it to push out any negativity that you don't want to be near you. For this, you'll need a combination of visualization and a moving mudra. Place your palms together with your fingers at right angles to each other and then rotate your palms against each other so that the directions of your fingers trade places. At the start, one hand will have fingers to the sky and the other will have fingers pointing forward. At the end, the positions of the hands will be reversed. This will make the chakram mudra generate energy.

As you move your hands, see energy surrounding you in your mind's eye. This part can be up to your ability to visualize and how your own natural energy pattern manifests, so it can vary. Some people may see a circle of brightly colored flame surrounding themselves. The flame can be any color at all. Some may see a bubble of energy or some other protective barrier. Visualize the barrier around your body becoming sharper and more intense. If there are colors, the colors become more vibrant. If there is a structure to your shield, it becomes opaque and substantial. The use of the mudra will aid the thickening of your shield, so you may find it becomes a bit larger too, and that's okay. In your mind's eye, see any negativity bouncing off your shield and returning harmlessly to the earth or its sender.

~6~
Healing

Spiritual healing is a meaningful and comforting addition to the natural healing of your body, when used in concert with regular medical intervention. Though mudras are no substitute for medical treatment, they are a gentle alternative healing method that will not interfere with the effectiveness of any medications. When using mudras for healing, take them into meditation or follow the more specific instructions found in this chapter.

Headache Begone Meditation

It is pretty hard to meditate when you have a headache, but it may be the best course of action. This meditation is a series of two hand poses, and the length of the meditation depends on the length of your headache. Ideally, start this meditation before the headache is full blown, such as when you feel pressure or vision changes that might precede a headache. As soon as you feel the inkling of a headache coming on, seek out a darkened room in which to meditate or turn down the lights as much as you like. This meditation is to be performed either lying down or seated with your hands resting on your lap. Begin with the keep it together mudra by pinching your index finger and thumb together, touching both hands at the pinch point, and then tenting and touching the rest of your fingers. Hold this position before the headache develops and you might be able to stave it off entirely.

If the headache develops further into pain, release the keep it together mudra and gently but firmly press the webbing between your index finger and thumb with both hands: your right hand will pinch the left hand and your left hand will pinch the right. Allow the rest of your fingers to relax loosely. Relax your shoulders. Relax your forehead. Allow the tongue to drop from the roof of your mouth. Remember to breathe. This hand pose is not a mudra per se, but it makes use of pressure points to alleviate or abbreviate headache pain. When the headache begins to subside, release the energy by touching the floor and visualizing any excess or negative energy flowing through the palms of your hands into the earth. Remember that mudras are no substitute for medical treatment.

Samputa Shadow Work

We all have personality traits that we wish did not exist. It is good to work on self-improvement to release bad habits and learn healthy coping mechanisms. Ultimately, nobody is perfect. Just as you crush one negative trait, another one might pop up. Furthermore, there may be some darker aspects of your personality that you can never fully destroy, remove, or transform. Most people keep those "shadow self" aspects hidden and repressed from everyone, even themselves. Shadow work is the spiritual practice of confronting your shadow self and learning from it. You won't be able to kill the worst parts of yourself, so shadow work can help you accept your shadow self in an appropriate way so that you can behave like the best version of yourself. It might seem scary to examine and tolerate, much less accept, your shadow self. However, the more you deny your shadow self, the more intense and powerful it becomes as it concentrates inside you, spilling out in ways that you don't understand and can't control.

Shadow work is best done through visions, such as dreams, so it is advisable to do shadow work before bedtime so that the work can continue in your dreams. If you're not used to having visions during the daytime, you can use tools that can help your mind's eye see what it needs to see in a process called scrying. Scrying is using something like a crystal ball, tea leaves, a candle flame, or a scrying mirror to allow images to come through the tool.

Often, just like in dreams, the images you see are symbolic, so don't be afraid if you see an image of something that is scary to you. Most of us are afraid of our shadow selves. Don't worry; scrying tools are not usually picture-perfect images of the future. For this exercise, I recommend using a very small mirror that can fit in the palm of your hand. The mirror will act as your scrying mirror to, hopefully, see visions of your shadow self. A mirror that comes with a small makeup compact is ideal and cheap to buy.

Careful preparation is needed for shadow work. First, prepare your space. Some people choose to cast a circle, which you can do using the Universal Rite from chapter 3. Find a safe-feeling space in which you will not be disturbed and cut out all distractions. Using only candlelight and burning incense can help create the random smoke and lighting that can aid your scrying as a beginner, allowing you to see things that you wouldn't see under ordinary circumstances. For additional ambiance, feel free to add some music that helps put you into a trance state.

Seat yourself and cup the mirror in the palm of your left hand with your right hand cupped over it in the samputa mudra. The samputa mudra represents all that you keep secret from others, and perhaps even yourself. You are conjuring your subconscious in the palm of your hand to view through your scrying mirror. Concentrate on asking your higher self to show you your shadow self. Press your hands together firmly and continuously apply pressure as you make your request of your higher self.

Focus on the sensation in your palms. Some people can feel spiritual energy as a temperature change, a feeling of prickling on the skin, or a "fuzzy" sensation. When you feel that you have pressed energy into the mirror (or after a few deep breaths if you're still learning how to sense energy), open your hands. Gaze into the mirror with soft, unfocused vision. Maintain your deep breathing and sit in meditation, focusing only on what you can see. When your attention wanders, bring it back to observation of what is happening in front of your eyes and in your mind's eye. You may have information pop into your head in the form of thoughts or sounds. Focus on dismissing the irrelevant thoughts and learning a message from your shadow self. Spend fifteen to twenty minutes in meditation.

When your time is complete, it is time to integrate this aspect of your shadow self back into your body. That's right—we're not going to throw away this piece of you, even if what you perceived was very negative. If you struggle with this part of the ritual, or you feel anxious about the process, pause to take a moment to reframe your shadow qualities as helpful or teaching qualities. For example, if you look into the mirror and see yourself looking old and ugly, allow yourself to see wisdom. If you see a fidgety, impatient person, allow yourself to see someone who is quick to try new things. If you see yourself frowning skeptically, allow yourself to see a person who always looks for a logical counterpoint to balance thoughts.

Cup your hand back over the mirror in samputa. Bring your hands to your chest and press the mirror against it, with the intention to integrate your shadow self more harmlessly into your life. Again, take a moment here to breathe deeply and try to sense the energy in your hands. As you breathe, ground yourself and know that the energies can be allowed to flow more freely in your body. It is thought that "stuck" spiritual energy can cause spiritual affliction and even manifest physical illness. By allowing your shadow self's energies to flow freely instead of being suppressed, you can lead a more spiritually healthy life.

Cleansing Your Life of a Codependent Toxic Person

You've learned a self-binding exercise already, and binding can also technically be used on others, but tying yourself energetically to a person is not always advisable. Think of a binding like buckling someone up in your car. You might do that for a child or other loved one, but you wouldn't want to hang out with an abuser in your passenger seat. Cutting energetic ties with someone is often the more pragmatic and healthy approach to dealing with a very negative person. Cutting ties with kartarimukha was introduced in chapter 3 in the section on soul retrieval because cutting ties is a necessary first step for soul retrieval. This section will go more in-depth into the act of cutting ties, since a very thorough job cutting ties may remove the necessity for any further magic or trouble with the person.

Beginning a thorough cord cutting starts with the most practical steps you can take, such as ceasing communication with the target person and removing or blocking all ability for future contact. It is okay if you want to tell the person one last time that you will not be contacting him or her and asking that he or she not contact you as well. You certainly don't have to reach out to say goodbye to a dangerous or harmful person, but if you choose to do so, make sure that all of your goodbyes happen before the cord-cutting exercise. Likewise, if you have any objects in your possession associated with him or her that you would like to rid yourself of or give back, make sure that those items are removed from your ownership before you do so. In some cases, destruction of some belongings that no longer serve you can aid in your magic. For example, if you ceremonially jumped over a broomstick when you were wed to someone that you must now cut out of your life after divorce, and you still own the broomstick, it can be broken or burned.

The magical part of cord cutting should be preceded with a spiritual bath or shower. Use the mrigashirsa mudra by cupping your hands and then extending your thumbs and pinkies. Pour water over your head with this mudra and scrub your body. As you do so, visualize your body being cleansed of any spiritual energies that are not your own. When your cleansing is completed, you are welcome to "dry off" by relaxing before the next step, the kartarimukha. It was described before in chapter 3, so this mudra will seem familiar to you. While seated or lying down in meditation, relax and visualize any remaining energetic ties with the target person. Many people visualize these ties as an umbilical cord, but others may visualize them as marionette strings. Allow yourself the freedom to see with your mind's eye how your energetic connections feel. Form your dominant hand into kartarimukha so that your fingers look like scissors. With your nondominant hand, touch the floor or furniture as a grounding measure. The energy can flow through any furniture or foundation to the earth, and the earth can harmlessly receive any residual negative energy that needs to exit your body. See yourself cutting the cords and allowing them to snap away from you like rubber bands.

When you have cut all the cords, give yourself a moment to check in with how you are feeling. Ground yourself and breathe deeply by continuing your contact with the earth through the ground or furniture and allowing any stuck or excess energy sensations to subside. As you breathe, concentrate on an energy exchange with the earth. When you are finished, you should feel calm but alert.

Any time you remove negative energy from someone or something, it helps to replace that negative energy with a blessing. The final step of this cord-cutting and cleansing ritual is to fill yourself up to the brim with blessings so that there is no more room for bad vibes. Use the self-acceptance (love) mudra by putting your hands in a prayer pose and then curling the finger of your right hand over the curled finger of your left hand. Spend a moment with this mudra, opening yourself up to a message from your higher self that can arrive as a thought, a feeling, or an omen.

When you have spent a few breaths in silent, receptive meditation, you have completed the entire exercise. In the majority of situations, what you have done will be sufficient to remove the influence of a toxic person from your life. Only in very rare cases would the connection return enough to require a soul retrieval. To perform the entire soul retrieval ritual, refer to on page 148.

Conclusion

Yes, mudras can bring greater grace, joy, and blessings to a union between two partners. But, as you've learned, the same mudras that are performed in temples and on stages can be used in simple greetings between kindred spirits. Now you can integrate mudras throughout your personal spiritual practice to bring your life grace. It is important to practice them frequently to remember them and to keep your hands in shape to be able to form them quickly and with ease. Look to your daily habits and see if you can enhance them with a flourish. For example, you could add a simple gesture to your first morning cup of tea to add a little magic to your day.

Mudras are ancient wisdom that need your help to continue to proliferate and heal the earth and fellow humans. Before video, there was very little recorded information of sacred historical dances. Some of the mudras you have learned were danced in temples a couple thousand years ago. Unless their magic is taught visually to others, it may become fundamentally altered beyond use or disappear entirely. So be the modern mudra magic maker. Practice mudras in your home, in your everyday precious moments and interactions. Spread those mudras in person, in photos, and in videos. The power is, has always been, and will always be in your hands.

Bibliography

Cunningham, Scott. *Wicca: A Guide for the Solitary Practitioner*. St. Paul, MN: Llewellyn Publications, 2004.

Grimassi, Raven. *Italian Witchcraft: The Old Religion of Southern Europe*. St. Paul, MN: Llewellyn Publications, 2000.

Kraig, Donald Michael. *Modern Tantra: Living One of the World's Oldest, Continuously Practiced Forms of Pagan Spirituality in the New Millennium*. Woodbury, MN: Llewellyn Publications, 2015.

Kynes, Sandra. *Sea Magic: Connecting with the Ocean's Energy*. Woodbury, MN: Llewellyn Publications, 2015.

Moura, Ann. *Green Magic: The Sacred Connection to Nature*. St. Paul, MN: Llewellyn Publications, 2002.

Sherwood, Keith. *The Art of Spiritual Healing: Chakra and Energy Bodywork*. Woodbury, MN: Llewellyn Publications, 2016.

———. *Sex and Transcendence: Enhance Your Relationships Through Meditations, Chakra & Energy Work*. Woodbury, MN: Llewellyn Publications, 2011.

Sherwood, Keith, and Sabine Wittmann. *Energy Healing for Relationships: Meditations, Mudras, and Chakra Practices for Partners, Families, and Friends*. Woodbury, MN: Llewellyn Publications, 2019.

U.D., Frater. *High Magic II: Expanded Theory & Practice.* Woodbury, MN: Llewellyn Publications, 2008.

U.D., Frater. *The Magical Shield: Protection Magic to Ward Off Negative Forces.* Woodbury, MN: Llewellyn Publications, 2015.

Recommended Reading

Carroll, Cain. *Mudras of India: A Comprehensive Guide to the Hand Gestures of Yoga and Indian Dance.* Philadelphia, PA: Jessica Kingsley Publishers, 2013.

Gutrud, Hirschi. *Mudras: Yoga in Your Hands.* Newburyport, MA: Red Wheel, 2000.

Saradananda, Swami. *Mudras for Modern Life: Boost Your Health, Re-Energize Your Life, Enhance Your Yoga and Deepen Your Meditation.* London: Watkins Media Limited, 2015.

Appendix

Ailment	Mudra
Allergies (no substitute for medical treatment)	Bramara (45)
Anger	Hridaya (34), Pasha (48), Keep It Together (73)
Bad Luck	Kartarimukha (12), Crossed Fingers, Pressing Thumbs (18)
Bullies	Empowerment (62), Keep It Together (73)
Chills	Surya (9)
Conflict	Mrigashirsa (25), Hansapakshika (28), Hridaya (34), Karkata (38), Pasha (48), Kilaka (49), Bherunda (20, 55), Atman (61), Keep It Together (73)
Crisis	Keep It Together (73)
Cursed	Sign of the Horns (26), Swastikam (39)
Danger	Pataka (8), Mushthi (18), Azabache (18), Mrigashirsha (25), Trishula (31), Vyagraha (32), Varaha (52)

Ailment	Mudra
Evil	Crossed Fingers, the Fig (18), Shikhara (19), Padmakosha (23), Kangula (23), Trishula (31), Swastikam (39), Shakatam (44), "No" (59)
Fear	Mrigashirsa (25), Simhamukha (26), Hridaya (34), Fearless (65)
Fever	Shankha (46)
Grief	Chatura (28)
Heart (no substitute for medical treatment)	Hridaya (34)
Hunger	Pushan/Biofeedback (77)
Hyperactivity	Hamsasya/Prana (11), Padmakosha (23), Dola (40), Shivalingam (43), Shankha (46), Body Integration (66), Hookup (70)
Impotence (no substitute for medical treatment)	Empowerment (62)
Impurity	Suchi (22)
Indigestion (no substitute for medical treatment)	Mukula (29)
Infection (no substitute for medical treatment)	Empowerment (62)
Infertility (no substitute for medical treatment)	Yoni (41), Shivalingam (43), Empowerment (62)
Insomnia (no substitute for medical treatment)	Khattva (54)
Instability	Kurma (51), Prana Integration (66)
Lack of Concentration	Adhachandra (14), Chandrakala (14), Sign of the Goddess (14), Azabache (18), Suchi (22), Triangle of Manifestation (56), Hookup (70)

Ailment	Mudra
Liver (no substitute for medical treatment)	Simhamukha (26)
Low Energy	Hamsasya/Prana (11), Arala (16), Alapadma (27), Triangle of Manifestation (56), Moon Altar (57), "Yes" (60), Trishira (75), Pushan/Biofeedback (77)
Low Self-Esteem	Mayura (13), Alapadma (27), Chatura (28), Tamrachuda (30), Anjali (36), Shivalingam (43), Samputa (50), Self-Acceptance (64), Soul Vibration (68)
Lungs (no substitute for medical treatment)	Simplified Mudra for the Lungs/Bronchial Mudra (33), Asthma (76), Pushan/Biofeedback (77)
Miscommunication	Samputa (50), Soul Vibration (68)
Memory Loss	Shikhara (19)
Nausea (no substitute for medical treatment)	Pushan/Biofeedback (77)
Needing Change	Ardhachandra (14), Chandrakala (14), Padmakosha (23), Kangula (23), Sarpashirsha (24)
Obesity (no substitute for medical treatment)	Shivalingam (43)
Obstacles	Ganesh/Patience (70)
Pain (no substitute for medical treatment)	Body Integration (66), Keep It Together (73), Abdominal Relief (74), Shankha (46), Pushan/Biofeedback (77)
Pelvis (no substitute for medical treatment)	Pushan/Biofeedback (77)
Poison (no substitute for medical treatment)	Simhamukha (26)
Poverty	Mushthi (18), Yoni (41)

Ailment	Mudra
Psychic Block	Hamsasya/Prana (11), Simhamukha (26), Sign of the Horns (26), Inner Vision (72)
Rash (no substitute for medical treatment)	Shankha (46)
Rocky Relationship	Ardhapataka (10), Azabache (18), Kapitta (20), Trust (68)
Sadness	Bliss (58)
Shadow Work	Samputa (50)
Spiritual Affliction	Hamsasya/Prana (11), Arala (16), Anjali (36), Bliss (58), Fearless (65), Body Integration (66)
Spiritual Bondage	Kartarimukha (12), Sarpashirsha (24), Sandamsha (29), Anjali (36), Kapotam (37), Swastikam (39), Pushpaputa (41), Ganesh/Patience (70)
Stagnant Energy	Shukatunda (17), Garuda (53), Empowerment (62), Trishira (75), Pushan/Biofeedback (77)
Stomach (no substitute for medical treatment)	Abdominal Relief (74), Pushan/ Biofeedback (77)
Throat (no substitute for medical treatment)	Shankha (46)
Underemployment	Tripataka (9), Tamrachuda (30), Bliss (58)
Unrequited Love	Mukula (29), Kapotam (37), Bliss (58), Soul Vibration (68)
Unsureness	Hamsasya/Prana (11), Padmakosha (23), Inner Vision (72)
Weakness	Chakram (47), Kurma (51), Garuda (53), Trishira (75), Pushan/Biofeedback (77)

To Write to the Author

If you wish to contact the author or would like more information about this book, please write to the author in care of Llewellyn Worldwide Ltd. and we will forward your request. Both the author and publisher appreciate hearing from you and learning of your enjoyment of this book and how it has helped you. Llewellyn Worldwide Ltd. cannot guarantee that every letter written to the author can be answered, but all will be forwarded. Please write to:

Dr. Alexandra Chauran
℅ Llewellyn Worldwide
2143 Wooddale Drive
Woodbury, MN 55125-2989

Please enclose a self-addressed stamped envelope for reply,
or $1.00 to cover costs. If outside the U.S.A., enclose
an international postal reply coupon.

Many of Llewellyn's authors have websites with additional information and resources. For more information, please visit our website at http://www.llewellyn.com